The
WONDERFUL WORLD
OF
CUSTOMER SERVICE
AT
DISNEY

2ND EDITION

BY
J. JEFF KOBER

A PUBLICATION
OF

J. JEFF KOBER

Published by Performance Journeys
Second Edition
10 9 8 7 6 5 4 3 2 1

Library of Congress Cataloguing-in-Publication Data on File
ISBN 978-1-62890-376-8

TABLE OF CONTENTS

PREFACE & ACKNOWLEDGEMENTS

WHY WRITE THIS BOOK?

The decision to write this book is rooted in many experiences. Some of my earliest memories were family vacations to Disneyland. I grew up watching *The Wonderful World of Disney* on Sunday nights. I was spellbound by how the magic was made. How did they create the *Happiest Place on Earth*? I simply had to know the secrets that made Disney great. That interest and love of Disney grew when Walt's son-in-law, Ron Miller, granted my request to tour the studios at Walt Disney Productions as a teenager. As I walked the corridors and back lots where classics like *Mary Poppins*, *The Love Bug,* and *The Jungle Book* were created, I became all the more determined to be part of the Disney magic.

Life experiences led me to believe that I needed a profession more stable than animation or film production. I was introduced to training and organizational development where I would labor for the next quarter century. But I still wanted to connect with Disney in some way. I appreciate the wise counsel provided by my professor, Stephen Anderson, regarding my graduate thesis at Brigham Young University: "Choose a topic you really love, because you have to live with it for a long time." As I pondered why I had gone through so many topics, I came to the conclusion that I really liked *Disney*. So my thesis and first publication were centered on Disney educational media.

It would be a few years and some valuable career opportunities creating organizational solutions for a number of corporations before I finally joined The Walt Disney World Company. It was great to be part of what would become the Disney Institute family, learning amazing insights from people like Judi Daley and other Disney leaders who modeled excellence. Unlike most people, who are assigned to work in a particular park or resort, my role was to benchmark all of Walt Disney World. My work encompassed the entire property. There I learned so much more than I ever could have learned behind a desk or in only one area of the operation. Many of those lessons formed the content that became *Be Our Guest*, prefaced by Michael Eisner.

But while I was excited that my programs became the core of the book, I was disappointed at not being its author. I was also disappointed by Disney business books written by outsiders who attended our programs, but really did not have the inside/outside view of Disney I had. Moreover, no one had the kind of experiences I had in helping outside organizations adapt these very ideas to their own location.

In time, I left Disney to embark on other consulting opportunities. As Chief Learning Architect of The Public Strategies Group, I focused on improving organizational performance at the federal, state and local level. Thanks to Lorraine Chang, Stephen Blair, Anne Teresa, Babak Armajani and Chuck & Mary Lofy for their mentoring and support as I transitioned out of my full-time experience with Disney. They were especially supportive in letting me bring my own unique experiences with Disney to other organizational settings.

With that mentoring I established my own consulting firm, Performance Journeys, and built a business sharing the lessons I learned from Disney and elsewhere. I've worked with Fortune 100 corporations, universities, hospitals, and other non-profit groups to create excellence through the lessons of Disney. Later I saddled up with my business partner, Mark David Jones. Together we've been able to continue celebrating Disney as well as other best-in-business entities through our current company, World Class Benchmarking. Here we have supported organizations with thought leadership and practical solutions in building great brands, creating high-performance cultures, and in establishing world-class results.

Still, I had a gnawing concern that no one had really done a thorough job of putting all of the wonderful stories about Disney together in a way that could help other organizations learn and grow. Finally, after years of being away from Disney, I came to a paradigm shift: I didn't have to be a current Cast Member to be the expert on Disney and best-in-business practices. I soon began to write online, and the response from readers validated my feelings. It's also allowed me to put together these stories in a way that can be brought to others.

So with the help of my colleague and illustrator Justin Rucker, plus reviews and edits from David and Leah Zanolla, I'm pleased to introduce the second edition of *The Wonderful World of Customer Service at Disney*. To all who read this, may you find not only ideas, but also hope and inspiration in adapting the lessons and experiences of Disney to create magic in your own organization.

And finally, my gratitude overflows to my family. As always, to my mother and father, Cora and Dale Kober, who believed in the power of a family spending time together. Most of all to my wife Kathy and my children: Mikell, Cameron, Braedon, Jennica, Madison and Preston. We've enjoyed (and even endured) so many visits to the parks. Kath has been an un-ending source of support and joy for so many years. To her, I may be no prince, but being a part of her life is as close to "happily ever after" as it gets. To her and all of my children, I dedicate this book.

See you at the parks,

Jeff

OVERVIEW

ENTERING THE TURNSTILES OF THIS BOOK

Welcome!

Before starting, a few key points:

1. If you haven't caught on to the preface of the book, let me say that I not only love Disney, but I think Disney is a great company to benchmark.

2. So in that context, The Walt Disney Company is a business. It must deliver bottom line profits. It has shareholders. It has a responsibility to bring in a profit and to address real world challenges.

3. Disney is imperfect. By no longer being a Disney leader, I can honestly discuss those imperfections--not to criticize the organization--but to help you see what you need do to improve your own organization.

What follows then are a number of lessons one can learn from Disney to apply to their own organization. In order to offer as much thought leadership to the topic of customer service, I have packed as many ideas as possible into the pages that follow. It isn't necessary to read this book in the order given, but there is some order to the book. Therefore, let me overview the sections that follow:

SECTION I: THE MIND OF SERVICE.

This section outlines the context, the philosophy, and the core of what makes a great Guest experience. Here you'll understand how quality has been tied to Disney's heritage. You'll see how understanding customers is foundational to providing great service. You'll learn about Disney's service mission as well as the four keys that are in place to make service succeed.

SECTION II: THE HAND OF SERVICE.

With a foundation in place, this section takes service in hand and makes it happen. In this, the largest section of the book, you'll find practical tools that create a great Guest experience. This section centers on operationalizing the customer service experience.

SECTION III: THE HEART OF SERVICE.

There is a spirit to service, one that can only be attained by individualizing the experience and making each Guest feel valued. It comes by really listening and empathizing with others. Without this important aspect, service simply becomes "serve us." I define a leader as one who serves with all their heart.

Mind. Hand. Heart. Great service will never succeed unless all three components are in place. That's at the center of this book, creating a total customer experience that truly delivers.

More than just a fun and insightful look at how Disney succeeds at customer service, this book is dedicated to helping you create real service improvements in your own organization.

SECTION

I

THE MIND OF SERVICE

THE CONTEXT AND PHILOSOPHY
FOR CREATING GREAT SERVICE

I THINK BY THIS TIME MY STAFF, MY YOUNG GROUP OF EXECUTIVES, AND EVERYONE ELSE, ARE CONVINCED THAT WALT IS RIGHT. THAT QUALITY WILL OUT. AND SO I THINK THEY'RE GOING TO STAY WITH THAT POLICY BECAUSE IT'S PROVED THAT IT'S A GOOD BUSINESS POLICY. GIVE THE PEOPLE EVERYTHING YOU CAN GIVE THEM. KEEP THE PLACE AS CLEAN AS YOU CAN KEEP IT. KEEP IT FRIENDLY, YOU KNOW. MAKE IT A REAL FUN PLACE TO BE. I THINK THEY'RE CONVINCED AND I THINK THEY'LL HANG ON ... IF ... AS YOU SAY ... WELL, AFTER DISNEY.

--WALT DISNEY

1

DISNEY'S HERITAGE OF QUALITY

QUALITY WILL OUT

Those are Walt Disney's words. But it didn't begin that way. Walt was simply trying to get an animation studio up and running. The *Alice's Wonderland* animated comedy shorts that he had done in Kansas City and was now producing in Los Angeles had waned. When Universal Pictures head Carl Laemmle wanted something different in the form of a rabbit, Walt quickly responded to the request by drawing designs for a new character. So earnest to please his client, he wrote: "If these sketches are not what you want, let me know more about it, and I will try again."

The feedback from the first hurriedly prepared Oswald the Lucky Rabbit cartoon was that the animation was jerky, and the character was dull. Walt went back to the table working long hours to inject more appeal into Oswald. Where cost-cutting measures like cycling the motion of the animation had been used by other artists, he resisted the temptation. Instead, he would review the rough animation, and send it back for improvements if needed. In time, his efforts paid off at the box office, where Oswald won warm reviews.

And they all lived happily ever after.

Well, not quite. Through contractual loopholes Walt lost control of Oswald the Lucky Rabbit. But that only made him more determined to make an even better character that people would embrace. And that character would become Mickey Mouse.

Since then, audiences have looked to Walt Disney for the finest in entertainment. In nearly every decade in the last century, audiences have headed to the local movie house to enjoy a favorite Disney film. And for nearly every decade in the twentieth century there was a Disney milestone that propelled Disney toward improving the quality of its cinematic experience.

In the 1920s, there was Mickey Mouse—the one who started it all.

In the 1930s, there was *Snow White and the Seven Dwarfs*.

In the 1940s, there was *Fantasia*.

In the 1950s, there was *Cinderella*.

In the 1960s, there was *Mary Poppins*.

In the 1970s, there was *The Small One*.

In the 1980s, there was *Who Framed Roger Rabbit*.

In the 1990s, there was *The Lion King*.

"Wait a minute!" you say. "*The Small One?* You mean the short where the donkey is carrying Mary to Bethlehem? What does *that* film have to do with quality? Most people haven't even *seen* that film!"

That little celluloid event was one of the most critical turning points in the Disney legacy of bringing quality to the screen. Up until that time, Walt Disney persisted in improving the work and quality of his films. But he died, and as a result, that passion for quality fell. So frustrated were many of Disney's own animators that, a day or two after the wrap party for the *The Small One*, director Don Bluth walked out of Walt Disney Productions with many of the animators to start his own company. He and the other animators claimed to be frustrated with the quality of the work and the conditions at Disney.

Bluth would go on to build his own reputation in animation with works like *An American Tail*, *Land Before Time*, and *Anastasia*. This key event and others like it shook the company to its foundations. In its wake, the leadership of Roy E. Disney, nephew to Walt and namesake to his father, labored to gather new executives that would, in time, reinvigorate not only Disney Feature Animation, but the entire Walt Disney Company as well.

"BUMP THE LAMP"

CEO Michael Eisner and studio chair Jeffrey Katzenberg came on board to revitalize the Disney organization and return the company to the level of quality so many had come to expect from Disney over the decades. While many projects were set in motion after that reorganization, one of the most ambitious was the film *Who Framed Roger Rabbit*. At this crucial point in the history of the Walt Disney Company, Eisner and Katzenberg signed on Steven Spielberg, Robert Zemeckis, and Richard Williams to do this unusual film. The project aimed to surpass even the best productions of its time.

To create the animation for this film, over 85,000 hand-inked and painted cells were created and combined with the live-action backdrops and actors, hand-animated tone mattes (shading), and cast shadows using optical film printers. No computer animation technology was available to create the animations—the technology hadn't yet been developed to that level. Some scenes involved up to 100 individual film elements. Any live-action to be composited later was shot in VistaVision to take advantage of the double-area frame of the horizontal 35mm format. All of this was done so the finished film would not suffer the increased graininess that plagued previous live-action/animation combos such as *Bedknobs & Broomsticks* or *Pete's Dragon*.

One of the places where the resulting quality of this careful hand-detailed animation can be seen is during the "Bump the Lamp" segment. If you've seen the film, you may recall that Eddie takes Roger Rabbit into the back room at the bar to cut apart the handcuffs that tie them together. In the excitement, the lamp from the ceiling is "bumped" and begins to swing. The shadows in the room exactly coincide with the lamp's swinging motion. This was an extra: the lamp did not need to be bumped for the storyline. In fact, a great deal

4

of extra work was needed to make the shadows match between the actual room shots and Roger's animation for what resulted in very little viewer benefit.

But this scene became a mantra for those laboring on the film. It was the moment Disney was going to depart from the more mediocre efforts of the past and "Bump the Lamp." Few viewers appreciate the subtle differences in shading that occur across Roger as the lamp moves and casts its shadows. In today's world, most would dismiss it as some computer effect if our attention were drawn to it. But there were no computers doing this kind of work back then. It is the quality of the detail in this effect and others that make the entire movie succeed.

In this cry for returning to quality, Michael Eisner created a welcome video for all attending Disney Traditions, the orientation program for new Cast Members. In this video, Eisner walks through the "Bump the Lamp" piece emphasizing that Disney is all about paying attention to the details others ignore.

In a short time, the expression "Bump the Lamp" was used by Disney Cast Members throughout the many divisions of the company. It became the notion of going that extra mile just to make something a little more special even though most viewers or Guests may never notice it. That welcome in Disney Traditions was used for several years after.

"USE EVERY PART OF THE BUFFALO"

About the same time the animator walkout occurred, another Disney animator was trying to make the case for taking animation to the next level. He became fascinated with the possibilities behind a moderately successful Disney film known as *Tron*, its only distinction being its rank as the first film to use extensive computer animation. The animator was fascinated by this medium and wanted to utilize it in animation as well. Unfortunately, Disney executives could not catch the vision and eventually let this cutting edge visionary go. His name was John Lasseter. His legacy? Pixar.

Fast-forward a few years. *Toy Story*, *Monster's, Inc.*, and *Finding Nemo* had already experienced great box office success. On this remarkable wave of success, John wanted to bring in fresh talent to keep the Pixar brand alive and to keep the quality strong. Brad Bird had experienced critically acclaimed success with *The Iron Giant*. He had been a classmate of John Lasseter in character animation school at CalArts—the California Institute of the Arts—in Valencia. And at one time, they were both working for Walt Disney Productions on *The Fox and the Hound*--the film that followed *A Small One*. Now Brad would direct a new Pixar feature called *The Incredibles*.

In Brad's own words:

> "When John Lasseter, Steve Jobs, and Ed Catmull talked to me about coming up here [to Pixar Studios in Emeryville, California] they said, 'We're worried about becoming complacent. We want you to come in here and kind of shake it up a little bit."[1]

> "For them to ask me to do that when they had nothing but successes was amazing to me."

Pixar wanted to take the studio to the next level. As Brad came on board, he created a mantra for making the movie the very best it could be. That mantra was placed on a light board above the entrance to his office. It stated: "Use Every Part of the Buffalo." Again, in his words:

> "Well the Indians—the American Indians—used to, when they killed the buffalo, they didn't just eat the meat. They ate the meat. They used the hide. They used the bones for arrowheads; they used every part of the buffalo. They didn't waste anything. So when I say "Use Every Part of the Buffalo" it means managing everything to get the most out of it."[2]

The Incredibles became a movie where everything was employed to create an over the top movie experience. From the story to the

---

[1] Brad Bird Interview from The Incredibles (Two-Disc Collection), 2004,
[2] Ibid.

characters to the animation to the voices and music, *The Incredibles* became, simply, incredible!

Disney has since acquired Pixar and together both studios labor diligently to create new animation milestones for succeeding generations. But they are not the only ones who can create milestones. We can *each* create milestones in our *own* organization that not only set us apart from our competition, but also win the loyalty of our customers.

QUALITY AND THE CUSTOMER

The name Disney is synonymous with great customer service. Yet Walt Disney never went into the customer service business. Initially he went into the cartoon business. But he knew over time he wouldn't be successful if he didn't create a quality product or experience. People often wonder if he would have liked a particular ride or Disney park attraction if he were still alive. I think he wouldn't be focused on rides and attractions. Walt Disney would be focusing on making the Internet easier to manage, or figuring out how to improve healthcare. He'd be focused on some of the very things you think about every day. Even when he passed away, he was trying to create the blueprints for a city of the future, which he referred to as EPCOT. Walt wasn't about customer service — he was about the customer — and in creating a better experience for people than could ever be thought imaginable. His success in the marketplace — and indeed, what drives the continued success of the Walt Disney Company today — was and is in the quality of delivering what people really want. For decades people have looked to the name Walt Disney for quality.

Your organization is probably not about cartoons, mice, or computer animation. But like Walt Disney, we can all bring quality to the work we do. Whether it's insurance, retail, or trucking, we can create excellence. Let's discover what that quality looks like at Disney, particularly with respect to customer service — but also to so much more.

CREATING YOUR HERITAGE OF QUALITY

LOOKING IN YOUR OWN MAGIC MIRROR, ASK YOURSELF:

- IS THERE A MANTRA — A CALLING CRY — FOR QUALITY IN MY OWN BUSINESS OR ORGANIZATION?

- WHAT IS IT ABOUT MY ORGANIZATION THAT INSPIRES QUALITY?

- WHAT ASPECTS OF OUR HERITAGE CELEBRATE QUALITY?

- WHAT DOES "BUMPING THE LAMP" LOOK LIKE IN MY ORGANIZATION?

- AM I PAYING ATTENTION TO THE DETAILS THAT EVEN MY CUSTOMERS OR EMPLOYEES DON'T NOTICE?

- HOW DO I "USE EVERY PART OF THE BUFFALO" IN MAXIMIZING MY RESOURCES?

- ARE WE ABOUT CUSTOMER SERVICE, OR THE CUSTOMER? HOW WOULD THAT REALIGNMENT IN FOCUS CHANGE THE WAY WE APPROACH OUR WORK?

2

CREATING THE EXPERIENCE

BUILDING DISNEYLAND

No one knew what Disneyland was all about. They thought it was simply another amusement park. But Walt saw Disneyland as something more than a theme park. It was more than a collection of rides and booths. He likened it more to going to the movies. But instead of watching the film, you stepped into the show and became part of the entire experience.

Van France noted that Walt himself had stated that Disneyland was not an amusement park, but rather a show played out on a large stage with the Southern California sky as a giant backdrop. Figuratively, Walt designed Disneyland like you were going to a movie theater. You begin with the outer lobby being the park's parking lot. The main gate of the park acts as an inner lobby. Here the ticket booths separate you from your money. You then enter a transition space, hallway or berm, where you leave the lobby and move into the theater. Even attraction posters were displayed promising attractions that were available to see, much as one would find movie posters in a lobby. Finally you enter the theater and the show itself, which is the actual park.

From there, you would step through the movie screen and experience it first hand. You would board the train around the park or listen to the band marching down the street. Everything you saw, heard and touched would be part of the experience. You could even go to the Main Street Cinema and watch an old-fashioned movie!

To support that experience Walt Disney added terms like Cast Member, to designate the idea that the employees were part of the large show being presented. The show itself is referred to as being on-stage. Cast Members when they are on-stage are in character, and their attending behaviors should reflect the show they are a part of. This would contrast to being backstage, where those behaviors and activities that would detract from the show would occur.

So the theme park experience would in many ways be similar to going to a theater. But here's the difference! Paying for admission into a Disney theme park is far more than what you pay to go to the movies, much less the nickel you laid down when you visited the Nickelodeon of yesteryear. The fact is—Disney's success is built not on film or rides—it's built on a total experience that engages the senses.

THE EXPERIENCE ECONOMY

Some years ago, B. Joseph Pine II and James H. Gilmore wrote a book called *The Experience Economy*, which discusses four different economic activities, based on the metaphor of getting a cup of coffee.

Commodities – In the time of Main Street, U.S.A., there was a market house where you would go and buy coffee beans by the pound, then take them home and grind them up. It was no more than a penny or two to buy enough beans to make yourself a cup of coffee.

Products – Someone came along a few years later and realized that they could make a little more money as a store if they ground the beans and then sold them in a can. Soon the local market had cans of fresh ground coffee. It costs a few pennies more per cup, but it was affordable.

Service – Along came the coffee shop. Why not just make coffee for folks and sell it to them? For many years a dime bought you a cup of coffee at the local diner. Today you can get it for about a dollar at 7-Eleven.

Experience – Then came Starbucks. Priced several times more than a cup of coffee at the gas station. In fact, adding organic soymilk to your latte is more than what a cup of coffee cost a few years back.

Why does Starbucks succeed?

In one's hometown, the experience of being in a Starbucks today is like being visiting your local tavern years ago. It was the place to hang out and to enjoy the company of friends and associates. Starbucks has come to replace Cheers (the bar from the 1980s TV sitcom), where "everybody knows your name." Starbucks became a hangout and one of the first places you could bring your laptop and use the Internet. It became the place for locals to meet up. From aroma to couches, people gladly paid for the experience of being at Starbucks. After all, it was simply cool to be at Starbucks. They even bought up the coffee-related merchandise. So successful was Starbucks that soon you could find one anywhere—from a strip mall to a palatial hotel in Dubai. So why not Disney?

DISNEY AND STARBUCKS

In recent years, Disney has decided to offer Starbucks in its parks. That should be an obvious fit—two great experiences together—right? Well...yes and no. The first Starbucks implemented was in the form of Fiddler, Fifer & Practical Café at Disney California Adventure. It was part of a new renovation of the park—one that had not yet successfully created the full experience for its Guests. Not only was the cafe new, but so was the entire boulevard. As an eatery near the central hub of the park, it was very spacious. Two major blocks of space were dedicated to queuing up for coffee and other Starbucks-branded foods. But the really great thing was an even larger amount of space available for patrons to grab a seat and enjoy—all in the setting of a California Walt might have first come upon when heading out West.

Somewhere between their coffee product and the opportunity of sitting down with friends and enjoying their coffee is where the heart of the Starbucks experience lies. This café provides all that. In fact there was

11

even more space outside if you enjoyed the weather—something Southern California does well. You should know that around 4 out of 5 people who visit Disneyland are from California. There are over a million annual passholders who frequently visit the Disneyland Resort. So this location does a great job of providing a place for friends to meet up while visiting the park. Its theming to another California era, and its views overlooking the plaza, fountain and Carthay Circle Theater all serve to create a great experience out of simply getting a cup of coffee.

Walt Disney World is a different experience. Starbucks at the Magic Kingdom is little more than Starbucks at the airport. You're purchasing taste and convenience—not an experience. Yes, it is themed to Main Street U.S.A. and yes, it carries all of the food and drinks associated with Starbucks. But there is no indoor seating, unlike its previous incarnation as a bakery. It was difficult to find a seat because the venue was so popular—not so much for the coffee as for the cinnamon rolls. But to accommodate what they expected to be queues of people lining up for coffee, they took out the tables and chairs.

Epcot's Fountain View carried the same format—a focus on queuing, but with the exception of some stand-around tables outside, there is little space dedicated to seating. Perhaps the thought is that there is a much smaller annual passholder crowd that would meet up like you would see in California. Thus the Starbucks at the Magic Kingdom, while very themed, is simply a quick-service operation. Is the Starbucks experience about being able to sit? No. But the Starbucks experience has largely been about what happens at those chairs and tables. It's about the interactivity, the conversation, even the needs that it satisfies—far and above satisfying hunger and thirst.

All that said, it was interesting when the fourth Starbucks opened, this time at Disneyland. Not only did its tight space offer plenty of accommodation for queuing, it provided for a wonderful little library on the side where Guests could sit and enjoy their drinks. Add to that a familiar pot-bellied stove, old-fashioned party line phones, and a checkerboard table.

Speaking of playing checkers, you can find this in several places at Disneyland and the Magic Kingdom. Spotted throughout are sets of checkers for people to sit back and enjoy. Why would anyone who has paid a fairly expensive price for a ticket into the park want to spend their time playing checkers when they could do that for practically free back home? Why would someone take that kind of time out of their day instead of seeing a one-of-a-kind billion dollar attraction you can't see anywhere else?

It's simple. Spend time and look at the people enjoying such experiences. Often it's a grandparent along with a grandchild. And though Disney works really hard to provide the most amazing rides and attractions, it's quite likely that the two sitting across from each other at that checkerboard experience may look back some 20-30 years later and remember with much fondness their moment playing checkers at Disney.

Coincidentally, it's chess—not checkers that people play at many Starbucks around the country.

What's all of this about? The message here is not about coffee, chess or checkers. It's about the experience. One that plays out again and again throughout the Disney experience, whether it's getting made up to look like a pirate at Pirate's League, meeting Goofy for the first time, or eating a five star meal at Victoria and Albert's.

You as an organization must decide—are you about commodities and products or service? Or are you really about the experience? There are successful organizations whose focus is around commodities and products and services—and yet they do well. Dunkin' Donuts has a fairly solid business model, but that is because it focuses on a different customer need than Starbucks. Still, I contend that the best opportunities—financially and otherwise—come in ultimately providing for the customer experience.

And how do you provide for that experience? That is really about understanding your customer's needs. And that's where we're going next.

CRAFTING YOUR CUSTOMER EXPERIENCE

LOOKING IN YOUR OWN MAGIC MIRROR, ASK YOURSELF:

- DO YOU PROVIDE COMMODITIES, PRODUCTS, SERVICES OR EXPERIENCES?

- WHAT WOULD BE THE ADVANTAGES TOWARD MOVING MORE TOWARD AN EXPERIENCE ECONOMY?

- WHAT WOULD IT TAKE TO MOVE MORE TOWARD AN EXPERIENCE ECONOMY?

- WHAT IS IT THAT YOU REALLY PROVIDE THAT OTHERS CANNOT EASILY REPLICATE? HOW DOES THAT LEND TOWARD THE EXPERIENCE?

3

UNDERSTANDING CUSTOMER NEEDS

Taking care of one's needs is what differentiates serving Guests serving customers. When we handle customers, we provide them with commodities, products and services. It no longer becomes a matter of serving coffee—but rather creating an experience that makes people feel cool. So in taking care of our customers, we must address their "true" needs—needs that may not necessarily be expressed in the context of fulfilling the request of a customer who wants to buy a used vehicle, or order the #3 combo with a diet soda.

In working with a wide variety of companies, I've come to understand that Guests have five fundamental, underlying needs. Fulfilling those needs takes what we do beyond providing a service to creating an experience. These five needs are as follows:

1. Be Heard and Understood

2. Belong and Contribute

3. Feel Stable and In Control

4. Feel Significant and Special

5. Be Successful and Reach Potential

Let's look at each of these to see how we ultimately serve a Guest experience rather than a customer experience.

1. BE HEARD AND UNDERSTOOD

To provide a great experience, you must first understand others. The first of the five human truths is the need to be heard and understood. Indeed, being heard and understood is an umbrella need that encompasses all of the other human truths. If we don't first seek to understand each other, we probably won't be able to address their other real needs.

Paramount is to first understand others before trying to get them to understand you. For example, before I would explain to someone a certain Guest Relations policy at City Hall at Disneyland, I would want to first make certain that I understood the real concerns of the individual. This makes sense. In fact, we've heard the same concerns so many times, it's easy to just jump right to the solution. But that would be a mistake. Even if we are clear as to what the issues are, we still need to listen empathically until the other person *feels* heard and understood. *Feeling* is at the heart of creating an experience.

Feeling understood requires that you sense emotionally where they are coming from. That doesn't mean that you have to cry along or act angrily if they behave so. But it does mean that you have to work with the individual long enough until they *sense* they have been heard. And that requires more than simply nodding along, or repeating what they said. It comes from taking time, asking open-ended questions, looking for examples, and aligning your understanding and response to what was really being said.

You can almost see a sense of resolve come over an individual when they feel they have finally been heard and understood. And it is from there that you can take action to support them.

2. BELONG & CONTRIBUTE

In the real world, it's called a time-share. At Disney Vacation Club, it's called *Vacation Club Ownership*. Why? Because owning or feeling like you are part of Disney is a big motivator for people to invest a large sum of money in real estate you only enjoy a small fraction of the year. As American Express says: "Membership has its privileges."

A fundamental human truth is the need to feel a sense of belonging and contributing. Belonging and contributing can happen in many ways. We belong in families. We establish friendships. We become part of a community. Even our national pride is a reflection of wanting to belong. You see it occur in diverse examples such as the following:

- Joining a street gang

- Cheering on your favorite team

- Losing weight in order to regain the lost romance in a marriage

- Spending too many hours at work in order to prove yourself

- Dressing in the latest, most popular and stylish clothing

- Enlisting in the armed services

- Facebooking or tweeting friends and even complete strangers online

- Joining the Rotary or Kiwanis Club

These examples, as widespread as they are, simply paint the picture that we all act in a variety of ways in order to feel like we belong and contribute to a community. Belonging and contributing gives people the courage to do something they might not do on their own. Conversely, it may also cause them to behave in foolish ways that they would have never previously considered. Understanding an individual's need to belong and contribute gives us perspective in better meeting the needs of those individuals through the products and services we offer.

3. FEEL STABLE AND IN CONTROL

Economic panic and instability in uncertain times is an easy way to understand why people need to feel stable and in control of their circumstances. But it's more than just how much is in your wallet. Providing stabilization can be manifested in all of the following ways:

- Purchasing a membership to a health club in order to get your waistline under control

- Being stranded in a terminal during a snowstorm awaiting word as to whether your flight is going to take off

- Taking out a life insurance policy in hopes of having some peace of mind

- Identifying the right day care program for your child in hopes that they are safe and kept from harm

- Requesting an open MRI so as to not experience the phobia of being in a tight, enclosed MRI scan

This same need plays out universally at Disney. Consider Disney Cruise Line. Like any cruise line, it reassures the safety of its passengers from the start by mandating participation in the muster drill. But a factor unique to Disney Cruise Line is the considerable number of children. So providing confidence that your child will be okay is important, whether it's an infant in the Small World or Flounder's Reef Nursery; a second grader wanting to spend all day in Disney's Oceaneer Club, a tween at Edge, or an "I'm too old to be supervised" teenager at Vibe. In each of these instances, parents trust Disney. And that trust gives them peace of mind that everything is safe and in control.

At its core, the experience of simply entering any Disney park around the world is rooted in the idea that you're leaving behind the uncertainties of the real world and entering a beautiful, warm, friendly environment. Therefore, Disney parks succeed to the degree that they can help you forget about your own troubles, but rather experience a utopian world of fantasy and adventure. Therefore, while admission to their parks is expensive, people are willing to pay that premium to experience that escapism. Things seem more consistent inside Disneyland than they do outside the park. Consistency leads to reassurance. In the real world you may drive by one beautiful building only to find next to it one in disrepair. This never occurs on Main Street, U.S.A. At Disney, it stays very predictable. In short, you trust it.

The real world is not about trust. You wonder how long the food has

18

sat out in the open on that food truck. You're never too sure about the wait at the Department of Motor Vehicles. And the Internet is filled with stories of hard and software companies that ultimately folded because they weren't tried and tested.

Trust and dependability are real needs.

4. FEEL SIGNIFICANT AND SPECIAL

Disney parks fulfill this need in amazing ways. Imagine arriving early at the Magic Kingdom and suddenly being invited by a Disney Cast Member to be *the* family of the day to be recognized with the mayor and citizens of Main Street U.S.A. above the Mickey Floral Portrait. Soon a train carrying Mickey and a host of Disney characters comes into the station to welcome you. You lead the crowd in a countdown, and soon fireworks explode behind you. Talk about feeling special!

Feeling significant and special is a powerful notion, and we devote time in this book to how Disney approaches that with their Guests. Here's just one example, however, of the price people pay to make their little one feel special. It's called Bibbidi Bobbidi Boutique. Here in a special location inside Cinderella Castle little girls are primped and made up into their favorite princess. It starts with hair and makeup, but soon moves into dresses, shoes, wands and tiaras. Add a special photo opportunity and soon you've spent a couple of hundred dollars on that little princess. And that doesn't include the admission into the Magic Kingdom. In fact, you could do the same thing at Downtown Disney without paying for the admission. But it wouldn't be the same as having it done at the castle.

Does your little girl feel special? Probably, but not as special as the parents *feel* about their little princesses. People pay a premium to make themselves and others around them feel special. A fundamental human truth is the need to feel important and unique. But not everyone can be king or queen of the day. What are some other ways to deliver to this need? Here are just a few ideas. They are simple—even low cost concepts, but powerful in fulfilling this need:

- Taking additional time to hear someone's concern, harking back to the first need we listed--feeling heard and understood.

- Writing a personal note to someone to let them know how much they mean to you.

- Adhering to the personal commitments you've made to another individual—however difficult they may be.

- Arranging for exceptions to policies and procedures to take care of individual needs.

- Rewarding and recognizing an individual's contribution in a uniquely meaningful way.

- Giving credit to someone who is often ignored.

- Sacrificing your will or opinion on a matter.

There are many ways that we can help someone to really feel significant and special. And there's a great feeling that comes with that opportunity to help others feel that way.

5. BE SUCCESSFUL AND REACH POTENTIAL

Remember our earlier discussion about Starbucks? This is why the Starbucks experience largely works. What made them a phenomenon across the country was that it became the locale to be seen and hang out in. It's where the "in" crowd hangs out. It's what separates a Starbucks from a Dunkin' Donuts. People are drawn to—and pay handsomely for—products and services that make them feel like they have arrived successfully in life. That's been the secret for many years with Apple computers. The message was that people who own a standard PC are dull losers. To be seen with an Apple product is simply much cooler.

Why is it important to understand people's need to experience growth and development? How can you help others reach for their fullest potential? People in general want to succeed. And with today's pressure to achieve, the thought that you might not be living up to your potential can become frustrating, even paralyzing.

What does success look like for others?

- Attaining adventure, love, fame, and fortune.

- Having courage to try new things.

20

- Refraining from the boredom of the status quo.
- Feeling the rush that comes with meeting one's goals.
- Seeing colleagues and loved ones reach their potential.
- Experiencing support from others in attaining their aspirations.

What keeps someone from reaching his or her potential?

- Dealing with difficult surrounding circumstances.
- Living with previous defeat.
- Being naïve.
- Lacking the vision of what could be.
- The possibility of pointing fingers, anger, or negative consequences.
- Feeling alone in your pursuits for something better.

Such a mentality is also very much at the heart of Disney. Mickey Mouse is the personification of the everyday man succeeding against whatever comes his way. *The Three Little Pigs* is more than a cartoon short—it's about a society getting past the throes of a major depression. Snow White, Cinderella, Belle and every princess story following in their footprints (or glass slippers) are about finding "happily ever after." Aladdin, Hercules and Wall-E? They're about the underdog succeeding. In film, we embrace success. And that success mentality plays out in everything else we do.

If it's about the experience, then we must meet the needs of our customers to assure that experience. It takes much more effort than selling an insurance policy, delivering a pallet of roofing materials, or replacing bandages on a patient. It means we know what they want, and exceed in our ability to deliver that service.

UNDERSTANDING YOUR CUSTOMERS

LOOKING IN YOUR OWN MAGIC MIRROR, ASK YOURSELF:

- WHAT CAN I DO TO BETTER LISTEN TO AND DELIVER TO MY CUSTOMER'S NEEDS?

- HOW DOES THE NEED TO BELONG AND CONTRIBUTE MANIFEST ITSELF AMONG THE SERVICE EXPERIENCE I PROVIDE?

- HOW CAN I ASSURE MY CUSTOMERS? HOW CAN I BUILD THEIR TRUST AS I SERVE THEIR NEEDS?

- WHAT MAKES MY CUSTOMERS FEEL SPECIAL? HOW CAN I CONSISTENTLY DELIVER TO THAT NEED?

- HOW DO MY PRODUCTS AND SERVICES ALIGN TO MY CUSTOMER'S VIEW OF SUCCESS?

4

EVERY GUEST A VIP

We've spoken about the idea that it isn't so much about customer service as it is about the customer experience. Now we'd like to address another idea—it isn't so much about the customer experience, as it is about the Guest experience. This chapter explores the difference.

BE OUR GUEST

"Be Our Guest" has been the invitation to Disney visitors long before the song from *Beauty and the Beast* became a box office hit. It underscores an important element in the Disney vocabulary, that Disney Cast Members are not to refer to customers as such, but rather as Guests. In fact, in the Disney nomenclature, the word "Guest" is capitalized and treated as a formal noun. To this end, another term Disney uses for its front line employees, besides Cast Members, is the idea of being a Host or Hostess.

What's the difference between treating someone like a customer, and treating someone like a Guest? What's the difference between being an employee and being a Host or Hostess? The obvious analogy is that we do things differently when we bring Guests into our home. We spruce up the house. We dress up. We prepare something special to eat. We host them. We meet and exceed their needs as they occur.

Disney hosts tens of millions of Guests in their parks and resorts each year. Are some more important than other? Let's look at what it means to be a VIP.

WHERE KINGS ARE COMMONERS…AND COMMONERS ARE KINGS

Since Disneyland opened in 1955, many important people have come from around the world to spend time in the parks. From kings, emperors, presidents and prime ministers, to the "I'm going to Disneyland/Disney World!" Super Bowl stars of today, celebrities have headed out to play at the castle. Walt Disney stated: "We love to entertain kings and queens, but the vital thing to remember is this—every Guest receives the VIP treatment."[3]

The interesting thing about these individuals is that they often want to simply be like everyone else when they visit. One such experience can be described with actress Betty Hutton's visit to Disneyland. From the moment she arrived, visitors recognized her and asked for autographs. So Miss Hutton determined that she would disguise herself. Heading over to Merlin's Magic Shop in Fantasyland, she purchased long false eyelashes, a buccaneer's hat and a special "sword" that went right through her head. The disguise worked perfectly; no one recognized the famous actress. But everyone stopped her to inquire where they could buy "a hat like that crazy one you've got on!"

I had the personal privilege of working closely with Judi Daley who, for over 30 years, was the official Hostess to almost every VIP, statesman, and celebrity who came to Walt Disney World. She exemplified the perfect ideal of a Disney Hostess. On her office walls were photographs of herself taken with five American presidents. If a celebrity needed to be taken care of, they called on Judi to look over their visit to Walt Disney World.

On one occasion I asked, of all of the people she had met, who had made the greatest impression on her or which experience had meant the most to her. She gave me the names of two individuals:

---

[3] Martin A. Sklar, *Walt Disney's Disneyland*, 1964. Disneyland Publication.

1. John Denver. Understand that, when most celebrities arrive, they come with an entourage of family, fellow performers, and support staff. Most are focused on the experience of the headliner. What stood out in her experience with John Denver was that he was more focused on whether the members of his band were having a good time, rather than on whether he was. For Judi, John exemplified the perfect idea of servant leadership—supporting those who support you.

2. Princess Diana. For the Princess of Wales, family was the most important thing. If there were a time when that was most important to Diana, it would probably have been just after her divorce from Prince Charles. Her boys were at a turning point of becoming teenagers, and she wanted to spend important one-on-one time with them.

Private time with her children meant getting rid of the paparazzi. So, while the Princess's complete entourage was spread out over an entire floor of Disney's Grand Floridian, Judi's role was to make sure that Diana had as much time away from the press and others as possible. Often that meant back dooring them into attractions or holding attractions over after hours. But the end result was that Diana was able to be just a mom spending time with her boys. And the paparazzi? They never got a single shot of Diana or the boys that entire week.

Just like the story of the Prince and the Pauper, kings really do want to be commoners. They simply want to be in control of their surroundings in a way that allows them to have the time they need with the ones they love the most.

Similarly, commoners want to be kings as well. Again, going back to our last chapter on understanding individual needs, people want to feel special. So Disney goes out of its way to make people feel special. Disney believes in treating everyday Guests like a VIP—Very Important Person.

VIP: A VERY INDIVIDUAL PERSON

The expression, VIP, can also mean a Very Individual Person. When we understand Guests and the essential needs they have, we become better at addressing them as individual persons.

Here's how Disney explained it in a 1975 Cast Member booklet[4]:

"Every Guest on our entire 42 square miles of property is a VIP whether they are visiting the Magic Kingdom for a day or vacationing in our resort-hotels for a week or more...Remember that 99% of our Guests are great people with everything going their way and having the time of their life. They are the easy ones to serve. Your real challenge will be that tiny 1%...the Guests who are hot, tired, hungry, confused, frustrated and perhaps missing their luggage, ticket books or cameras. Or perhaps all of the above. They may not be very understanding and it may be up to you to turn their day around into the positive kind they came here to experience."

Individually focusing service toward that tiny 1% Disney talked about is a great way to treat Guests like VIPs. That's why it's important that we understand the real needs of our Guests and walk in their shoes to provide the best experience possible. When we serve from the perspective of understanding their journey, we find our Guests are extremely satisfied with the services we provide.

Let's talk about paying attention to that 1%. While we can't individually serve the remaining 99%, rest assured they are watching us, observing our treatment of the 1% and making silent judgments about how we would treat them as well. When we are extra patient with the 1%, when we go out of our way for the 1%, when we stay calm, cool and collected with the 1%, it speaks volumes to the 99%.

Curiously, such observation is not unlike my own experiences working with zoos. How the zoo took care of its animals often became a silent commentary about the kind of extended effort the zoo made towards the Guests visiting the zoo. And visa versa. The way you treat your zoo patrons spoke a silent sermon on how well the zoo paid attention to its animals.

---

[4] *Your Role in the Walt Disney World Show*, Internal Publication, Walt Disney Productions, 1975

THE GOLDEN RULE & THE PLATINUM RULE

Our opportunity as service providers is to deliver a VIP experience to our Guests. That requires understanding the *Golden Rule* and the *Platinum Rule*.

What is the *Golden Rule*? It's doing unto others as you would have done to yourself. It's a good service philosophy. But the better experience comes via the *Platinum Rule*. What is the *Platinum Rule*? It's doing unto others as they would have done unto themselves. When we meet the real needs of others as they would have them met, we have attained platinum-style service.

A simple example of this is that if you had Guests at your home, would you assume that everyone drank chocolate milk like you and thus, serve him or her chocolate milk? Obviously no. Just because it's your favorite drink doesn't mean that it's theirs.

Let me give you a more involved example of what that means. On one occasion I had flown late one weekend afternoon into the Sacramento airport. I had been in New York for the last week providing programs, and it would be several more days before I would be home again. All I wanted was to get my rental car, head to my hotel, and get some rest.

I got in line to rent my car. There were only 3-4 people ahead of me, waiting for one of two people running the desk. Yet it was 25 minutes before I finally got to the front of the line. All that was running through my head was, "What is taking so long?" I soon found out why. Not only were their computers running slowly, but also the young lady I met was the friendliest person I had ever met. She asked about me, asked if I had been to Sacramento before, asked where I was from, and when learning it was Orlando, asked about the lifestyle of living in Florida. She was as friendly and kind as anyone could ask for in a customer service relationship. Only I didn't want a new friend—I wanted a car! Can you see how it's really about service by the *Platinum Rule*—not service by the *Golden Rule*.

This went on for a few moments when out of nowhere a manager came out from the back room. She saw the line of people waiting for their car, and then after grabbing something from behind the counter, started heading back toward her office.

"Don't you go back there!" I couldn't believe the words came out of my mouth.

"I waited nearly half an hour for a car, and there are still others behind me waiting for theirs. You should be working the counter!"

The manager stopped in her tracks. Then slowly, she motioned toward a computer console. After typing a few keystrokes, she invited a customer to the counter.

After a few moments, the manager had to go to the back room to grab a set of keys. As she did, the young employee assisting me with my rental leaned toward me and whispered, "I'm glad you told her to help out!

I could write a volume regarding that experience at the car rental counter that afternoon. Let me especially note the following:

1. Would you be back in your office or bedroom if you were having Guests to your home? No. You would be out in front with them. That's the difference between customers and Guests.
2. If you were attending to Guests at home, and you needed help, would you ask other members of your family (in this case, fellow employees) to help you out? Would you put your Guest on hold while you did other things?
3. If you knew your Guest was really needing and wanting to leave, would you stop and chatter, or would you make certain your Guest was on their way as quickly as possible?

Focusing on the Guest is simply different than focusing on the customer, much like focusing on the experience is more involved than simply providing service. Therefore, the rest of this book is not so much about customer service, but about taking it to the next level in improving the Guest experience.

Having identified that it's the Guest experience we must focus on, let's take it to the next level by talking about great Guest experiences, and not just good Guest experiences.

MAKING EVERY GUEST A VIP

LOOKING IN YOUR OWN MAGIC MIRROR, ASK YOURSELF:

- HOW CAN I TREAT OTHERS LIKE THEY ARE GUESTS RATHER THAN CUSTOMERS?

- HOW DO I TREAT OTHERS LIKE A VERY IMPORTANT PERSON?

- HOW DO I TREAT OTHERS LIKE A VERY INDIVIDUAL PERSON?

- HOW DO I PAY ATTENTION TO THE 1% THAT REALLY NEEDS EXTRAORDINARY SERVICE?

- HOW CAN I EMPHASIZE THE PLATINUM RULE IN MY ORGANIZATION?

5

PROVIDING GREAT GUEST EXPERIENCES

WHAT TIME IS THE 3:00 PARADE?

Think about it. You're a Magic Kingdom Cast Member picking up trash and a Guest comes along and asks, "What time is the 3:00 parade?"

Believe it or not—the question is asked more often than you might think. But what does it mean? More important, what is your reply?

Before we answer those questions, let's set the context. The 3:00 parade at the Magic Kingdom at Walt Disney World is one of the park's most attended attractions/events. More people experience that parade than set sail in Pirates of the Caribbean or take flight in Space Mountain. Thousands of Guests crowd the parade route and there's a lot riding on that experience for them.

What's more, it's the middle of July. You've been outside nearly the entire day. It's edging close to 100 degrees and the humidity is pretty much aligned to that same number. You've just finished picking up trash that has a smell you can't quite describe, but it has squelched your need to eat something on your long overdue break. And now some Guest has asked you, *"What time is the 3:00 parade?"…!*

What does that question really mean to the Guest? What is your answer?

CONNECTING EMOTIONALLY TO CUSTOMERS

Remember that at some point during their stay, Guests must connect (or reconnect) *emotionally* to Disney by meeting and exceeding one of those five needs. For newcomers, it may be that first moment they set eyes on Cinderella Castle. For some individuals, it's a meet-and-greet with Mickey Mouse or their favorite character. Others may connect emotionally through a magical moment with a Cast Member. But if they haven't had that moment by *3:00 in the afternoon,* you want to make sure it happens before the parade passes by. Literally. That's because there's a lot of Guests that head right out of the park after the parade. Some go back for a swim at their hotel and return later on. But many of them leave and don't come back. So it's critical that there's an emotional connection with the Guests before they head out that gate.

Therefore, so much depends on the 3:00 parade. That's why Disney works very hard to make the 3:00 parade as special as possible. This includes the following measures:

CREATING GREAT GUEST EXPERIENCES

Considerable design and preparation go into the creation of the parade. The 3:00 parade may only be changed out every 6-7 years because the average Guest will only see it once or twice during that time. At Disneyland and Tokyo Disneyland, the parade changes out much more often because they draw more on local crowds that return regularly. Creating a parade that can be shown day after day requires great attention to the building and upkeep of floats. It requires the sewing of hundreds of costumes as well as the upkeep of those costumes. New music is written and recorded. A large staff of performers is hired, with training and choreography beginning weeks prior to the first step on the parade route.

Beyond this, there's enormous groundwork that goes on each and every day. Let's look at what it takes.

READYING GREAT GUEST EXPERIENCES

From the moment you arrive you are reminded of the 3:00 parade. Your tram Hosts will talk about it while escorting you from the parking lot to the Transportation and Ticket center. Park brochures and tip boards announce it. Even your Jungle Cruise skipper will joke about it while waiting to re-dock.

In the hour prior, preparations are underway along the parade corridor. Signage is posted. The route itself is lined out with rope or tape. To ensure that the parade route is properly staffed, Cast Members from throughout the park are utilized to support Guest control before, during, and after the parade. Even the supremely important policy of staying in your themed area with your themed costume is suspended for purposes of supporting the parade. Therefore, it's no surprise to see a Tomorrowland Cast Member helping Guests along Main Street.

Cast Members will interact with Guests by inviting them into games of jump rope or efforts to perform the "wave." The intent is to not only pass the time away or keep Guests from leaving, but to connect 1:1 with the Guests. Fifteen minutes prior to the parade's starting time, The Walt Disney World Band will file through the route to help prepare and clear the parade route.

While you're busy watching this, you may not notice that windows are opening along Main Street, Liberty Square and Frontierland. These windows open electronically in preparation for the parade. Behind these openings, speakers are in place. When the parade concludes, wait a few minutes and you will see these same windows quietly closing.

DELIVERING GREAT GUEST EXPERIENCES

When the parade comes through, it must be an emotional "wow" for the Guests. Again, technology supports this. To create a tight, emotional experience, the parade is directed from a small room underneath Peter Pan's Flight. Adjacent to where rides and attractions for the entire Magic Kingdom are monitored, the small cubicle contains both video images as well as electronic images of the parade passing through. It is from this hidden location that parade float drivers are directed to slow down or speed up their paces. It's what keeps the parade from falling apart.

Meanwhile, upstairs, there is a wonderful, dedicated group of Cast Members who work their hearts out to bring magic into the parade. Most of them are young, but not all. Many came to work in the parade because they themselves were connected emotionally to the Disney experience when they were younger. Now they give back with everything they have. Keep an eye on those that are "face" characters. Look how they give eye contact to so many along the route.

All of this combines to create an amazing Guest experience. If you watch the Guests, you will see that a great many leave feeling the "pixie dust." A lot of Guests simply line up behind the parade and join the procession.

CONTRIBUTING TO GREAT GUEST EXPERIENCES

So let's back up. It's another 45 minutes before the parade starts and someone approaches you as a Cast Member and asks, "What time is the 3:00 parade?" What do you say? I'll give you a hint: The answer is not "3:00."

For one thing, consider that the parade begins on one end of the park in Frontierland, and then moves to Liberty Square, up in front of the castle, and on down Main Street. It actually takes the better part of an hour for the parade to completely wind through its route. The question on its own has merit.

But the appropriate answer lies in understanding the Guest. This is a chance to provide a one-on-one experience for the Guest. What we really want to do is to think why the Guest is asking the question in that manner. Then we want to respond appropriately. Perhaps the Guest wants to go on more rides and wants to watch the parade as late as possible. Maybe the Guest is looking for a place to sit down, or a place in the shade during the parade. Perhaps the Guest is looking for a place where it isn't crowded so their children might be able to see.

33

You have to take time and inquire. You might ask: "Well, where are *you* planning to be at that time?"

They might reply, "We were going to head over to The Barnstormer Starring the Great Goofini if we had time." Your response might be, "Okay then, perhaps you might want to take the train just before 3:00 p.m. and stake out a place near Town's Square. There'll probably still be some good places to see the parade without having to wait too long."

To that stroller mom who wants complete control of the day's itinerary, that's so much better than simply stating "3:00 o'clock." It fulfills a real need to make everything about their day as perfect and successful as possible.

As you inquire about the Guest's needs, you notice that their little one is dressed up like Ariel. You get down at the same level as them and ask about her favorite princess. You then get her excited about the fact that Ariel and Prince Eric will be in the parade. You teach her how to wave like a princess, and where to stand so that Ariel can see her when the float comes by.

Standing up again, the grandfather notices that your Cast Member nametag says that you're from Norfolk, Virginia. He mentions his naval service for many years in Norfolk. You mention that your dad was also transferred to Norfolk while in the Navy and that's where you were born and spent much of your childhood. You develop a quick connection as you discuss your shared hometown.

Again, it's not about telling people the parade time. It's about meeting and exceeding one or more of those five needs we spoke of earlier.

Of course, this book isn't just about Disney. It's about *your* business as well. So ask yourself: "What is *my* 3:00 parade question? What is the obvious kind of question *my* customers ask, and what does it mean in terms of providing a great guest experience?"

Also, what is your 3:00 parade moment? In other words, what is the one emotional moment where you can connect to your customers? When is the moment they become emotionally connected to you?

How do you create, anticipate, and carry through that 3:00 parade moment in your organization so that it can come alive each and every time it happens? How do you train your employees not to answer the obvious, but rather seek to understand your customers?

Every business can and should have its own 3:00 parade moment. It's the opportunity to connect with others in a way that makes your business stand out. Look for it. Maximize it. And prepare your customers for an experience that will cement their loyalty to your organization.

PROVIDING GREAT GUEST EXPERIENCES

LOOKING IN YOUR OWN MAGIC MIRROR, ASK YOURSELF:

- WHAT IS YOUR 3:00 PARADE QUESTION? WHAT NEEDS ARE BENEATH THAT QUESTION?

- HOW DO I EXCEED CUSTOMER EXPECTATIONS BY UNDERSTANDING OUR CUSTOMER'S NEEDS?

- HOW DO I PREPARE THE CUSTOMER EXPERIENCE TO BE A POWERFUL AND POSITIVE EMOTIONAL MOMENT?

- IS EVERYONE ON BOARD ABOUT DELIVERING A GREAT CUSTOMER EXPERIENCE? AM I ON BOARD?

6

GETTING EVERYONE ON BOARD WITH SERVICE

We've covered several key points by now:

- It's about standing apart—it's about quality.
- It's about the experience, not the commodity, product or even the service.
- It's about really meeting the needs of those you serve.
- It's about Guests not customers.
- It's about treating people as VIPs by providing Platinum level service.

In short, you know that you want to provide great Guest experiences. But how do you get everyone to contribute to that goal? If you want to create an organization that is perceived as having a solid Guest-centric culture, you must get everyone on board to the notion that the Guest experience is paramount to the long-term success of the organization. Indeed, with every employee you hire, you must focus on the pivotal role of customer service starting on the first day they are hired, to the last day of their employment with you. How do you do that? You begin by getting everyone to work off the same page.

WE CREATE HAPPINESS

Imagine you could have any role at Disneyland...What job would you want?

You could be a conductor on The Disneyland Railroad, clean restrooms, sail rafts across the Rivers of America, or serve hot dogs. You could be "best friends" with Mickey Mouse, or wave to others in the parade as a princess. You could be an Imagineer creating attractions, or even the President of the entire Disneyland Resort. No matter what job you choose, even if you are the new CEO of the Walt Disney Company, you will attend a classroom orientation known as Disney Traditions. During this orientation you will learn the mission of the company and what your number one priority is. That priority can be stated in just three words:

"We Create Happiness."

That's what it was in 1955 when Dick Nunis and Van France created Disney Traditions. The mission is a little longer now. In 1971, it was changed to: "We create happiness by providing the finest in entertainment."

It changed again in 1990: "We create happiness by providing the finest in entertainment to people of all ages everywhere."

But when you're teaching an 18-year-old Cast Member what their job is, it's easier to say simply, "We create happiness."

What does that mean?

POP...BOX...SELL

Let's consider an 18-year-old popcorn seller: the role of this individual is to pop popcorn in front of the castle. All day long, that's his job. Pop the popcorn. Box the popcorn. Sell the popcorn. Pop, box, sell. Pop, box, sell. Pop, box, sell...day in, day out. From park opening until closing, and with the park open 365 days a year, it can feel like *Groundhog Day* all over again.

Imagine that this Cast Member is at his cart, popping popcorn. In between taking care of Guests he notices two older ladies taking a picture of each other in front of the *Sleeping Beauty Castle*. While standing there, what could he do?

You got it! Take the picture so that both ladies could be in the picture.

He approaches and asks if they would like him to take a picture of the two of them together. They respond that they would appreciate it, so he takes their picture in front of the castle. They thank him and he goes back to popping popcorn.

Has he created happiness? Has he provided great customer service?

Sure. But now consider that some three months later, one of those two ladies writes a letter to the park's management and shares the following:

> To whom it may concern:
>
> A few months ago my sister and I went to Disneyland together. While there, the popcorn seller by the first name of so and so stopped to take a picture of both of us in front of the castle. Please see a copy of the enclosed photo.
>
> What the popcorn seller didn't know was that my sister and I had not been on speaking terms for some 20 years. When I learned that she was facing chemo for cancer, we made amends by coming to your park and spending some time together. The picture you see enclosed is now the only one taken of us together in some 20 years. I'm so grateful for the young popcorn popper who took the time to take the picture. I will be indebted for having this last memory.
>
> Sincerely yours...

Did the popcorn seller "create happiness"? Yes! And why? Because an 18-year-old popcorn seller was taught to do more than his task. He was taught to fulfill the mission of the organization—in this case "creating happiness."

POINTED IN THE SAME DIRECTION

It's important to have everyone working toward the same mission. Returning to the true scenario we just illustrated, imagine now a fictitious experience where the popcorn seller returns to his wagon only to see a manager waiting impatiently. The supervisor snaps: "What are you doing?"

"I noticed two ladies taking a picture of each other and so I thought I might make it possible for them both to be in the picture."

"That's not your job."

Nervously the 18 year old defends himself: "Well, there really wasn't anyone buying popcorn and I just thought it might be kind of a nice gesture. After all, aren't we supposed to create happiness?"

"I don't want to hear about that happiness crap. Look, your job is to pop the popcorn. If I see you stepping away from this wagon when it's not your break, I'm writing you up. Now get back to your job."

What do you think that popcorn seller is going to do next time there's someone taking a picture of the rest of his or her family? You can bet he'll think twice before offering to take a picture for them. For that matter, you can imagine that, after that kind of response, your popcorn seller is going to conclude: "Forget it...I'm just going to do my job and get out of here. Hopefully I can get a real job real soon—somewhere else!"

The story with the popcorn seller and the two elderly woman really happened. The follow-up experience between the popcorn seller and the manager fortunately did not. But it points to the fact that a powerful service vision like "We Create Happiness" only works if everyone— including those at the top—is pointed in the same direction.

"We Create Happiness," a concept built by Dick and Van when Disneyland was first created, has endured until today. By shaping a vision in your own organization, you can build an ideal, a statement, that exemplifies the products and services you offer. In their landmark book *In Search of Excellence*, Tom Peters and Robert Waterman wrote:

> "Whether or not they are as fanatic in their service obsession as Frito, IBM, or Disney, the excellent companies all seem to

have very powerful service themes that pervade the institutions. In fact, one of our most significant conclusions is that, whether their basic business is metal-bending, high technology, or hamburgers, they have all defined themselves as service businesses."

Imagine the possibilities, even the power when everyone is pointed in the same direction with the same higher purpose in mind! It's attainable even in your kingdom, just as it is in this happiest of all places.

GETTING EVERYONE ON BOARD

LOOKING IN YOUR OWN MAGIC MIRROR, ASK YOURSELF:

- DO I HAVE A SUCCINCT DECLARATION OF MY ORGANIZATION'S PURPOSE?

- DOES IT COMMUNICATE A CLEAR EXPECTATION INTERNALLY OF WHAT MATTERS MOST?

- DOES IT CREATE AN IMAGE OF MY ORGANIZATION?

- IS IT MORE THAN A CORPORATE MISSION STATEMENT NAILED TO THE WALL IN SOME BOARDROOM?

- IS EVERYONE ON BOARD WITH THAT MISSION? HOW DO I GET CO-WORKERS ON BOARD WITH THE MISSION?

- HOW DOES MY ROLE TIE INTO THE MISSION OF THE ORGANIZATION?

7

DISNEY'S FOUR SERVICE KEYS

OPERATIONALIZING SERVICE

In the last chapter we noted the experience of creating happiness when an 18-year old popcorn seller took the time to take a picture of two older women so they could be in the picture together. We also spoke of the effect had when others are not cohesive with the same mission. The example given was that of a manager citing the same employee for not staying at his popcorn wagon and selling the popcorn.

After Disneyland opened, Van France left Disneyland to embark on adventures elsewhere. A few years later he returned to work at Disneyland, this time reporting to Dick Nunis, whom he had originally hired years earlier.

In walking through the park, he came to realize that there was a definite reality gap between the romance preached at The Disney University, and what was really happening out in the trenches. A new hire's first few days were filled with excitement about working at Disneyland, about being part of the show as a Cast Member, and about the importance of creating happiness. Reality would then sink in. Typically, a foreman would welcome them "to the real world." Different terms would describe the working realities of the job. One Cast Member assigned to the cars at Autopia would hear, "Welcome to Blood Alley!" in reference to the demands of working with engines, smoke, and the possibility of being run over by youngsters driving cars. Back then there was no center rail, and kids were driving all over the track.

Clearly everyone in the park needed to be on the same page, and the mission needed to extend past the orientation. One of those initiatives was the development of a program that would operationalize on that service vision. It was entitled,

"SAFETY...COURTESY...SHOW...CAPACITY."[5]

Though "capacity" was later changed to "efficiency," these standards have endured the test of time. Whether it's a hotel operation, a food and beverage outfit, a recreational location, or a thrill ride, these standards find their application throughout the parks and resorts.

THE GUEST EXPERIENCE AT THE HAUNTED MANSION

Let's look at an example of great customer service using one of the most popular attractions in any Disney theme park, the Haunted Mansion. For those who have visited this attraction, you wouldn't think that a strong example of building on customer service standards would emanate from a ride attraction that focuses on being dilapidated and scary. You would think a better example might come from a high-end experience like Club 33 at Disneyland or Disney's Grand Floridian Resort at Walt Disney World. But it's the fact that those standards still are emphasized in what is otherwise a carnival-type spook alley attraction that makes it all the better an example for study.

So let's examine how Disney applies its standards to one of the most foreboding places in the Magic Kingdom:

Safety. Safety is priority number one among all Disney standards. It's important that the park not only be designed with the safest possible conditions, but that Cast Members be the eyes and ears of the Guests to help protect them from possible accidents and mishaps. An unofficial axiom among Cast Members (especially those associated with attractions like the Haunted Mansion), is the very unofficial, "A dead Guest is not a happy Guest."

---

[5] Van Arsdale France, *Windows on Main Street.* 1st ed. Livonia: Stabur Press, Inc.

Courtesy. While in the spirit of a spook alley attraction like the Haunted Mansion, Cast Members may suspend what Walt Disney World is known world wide for—friendly customer service. But in general this plays out as Cast Members treating each Guest individually. Service behaviors such as greeting each and every Guest—even with goulish delight are part of this. So is focusing attention on children, all contribute to being Courteous. Making sure needs for those with physical and other challenges are met is a requirement—even at the Haunted Mansion.

Show. The Haunted Mansion reinforces the importance of the Show in its myriad of details. It's displayed in its stories, architecture, animatronics, music, lighting, and special effects. From Madame Leota to the sounds of *Grim, Grinning Ghost*, there is much in the show that captures you and draws you into what is the quintessential Disney attraction.

Efficiency. This was originally listed as Capacity. In time, the term was changed to Efficiency to capture a broad array of organizational issues. With tens of thousands of Guests going through the parks each day, Efficiency is critical to the success of the operation. In the Haunted Mansion it plays out not only with the continuously moving ride vehicles, but in the duplicate sets of stretch rooms that continually feed Guests to the ride portion of the attraction.

APPLYING AND PRIORITIZING SERVICE STANDARDS

These standards are critical to the Disney experience that Guests receive. Let's see an example of how these standards play out:

You are a Cast Member at the Haunted Mansion, costumed in a cloak of deep forest green. Your role is to assist Guests in boarding their "doom buggies" as they continue their journey into the dark abyss. You walk continuously backward on the moving platform, encouraging Guests to "watch your step." After repeating this activity for some duration, you look up only to find that no one is boarding. In surveying the queue, you notice that the entire line is held up for an elderly gentleman with a cane. You have a few options:

1. If efficiency is your biggest priority, you could holler: "Get out of the way, you're holding everybody up. Keep moving along people!" Of course, that would be throwing courtesy to the wind, not to mention doing little for safety or show, but it would be efficient.

2. You could stop everything and put on a little show, giving the elderly man a complimentary death certificate and declaring him "most likely to be the next permanent occupant of the Haunted Mansion." It might make for interesting Show, but the elderly individual might take offence, and it would create for a very inefficient operation.

3. You could press the button to bring the ride to a stop, assisting the elderly gentlemen in boarding his "doom buggy." It would showcase your commitment to Safety. And it would be a great act of Courtesy.

Obviously, item #3 is the appropriate choice, and the one that should be played out all the time at the Haunted Mansion. If I, as a manager, notice the ride has come to a stop, I would follow up with the front line Cast Member and ask how he or she made the decision. If that decision was made in the context of a set of prioritized standards, then I know I have taught the Cast Member how to make decisions within the correct framework.

The only downside is that for everyone experiencing the attraction, they too would come to a stop, and begin wondering whether the attraction had stopped operating. This is an example of where management approaches these standards strategically. It would not be safe if Guests began to wonder if the ride had ended and they began to try to get out of their ride vehicles. Also, it ruins the theming if, out of safety and courtesy, they just announce: "The ride has stopped. Remain in your vehicle." Instead, Imagineers and operators created a solution that works within the framework of those standards. Instead of a boring, rote recording, the following is stated by a haunted voice within the mansion: "Prankish spirits have interrupted our journey. Please remain in your Doom Buggy."

In short, we *can* operate tactically and strategically within the framework of a given set of service standards. Indeed, the example is really fictional, because someone with a walker would be escorted to another location that would require less walking and would more easily accommodate their boarding the doom buggy.

These four keys play out elsewhere around the Haunted Mansion. Here are some examples:

The Greeter – The greeter at the entrance to a ride and attraction such as the Haunted Mansion plays a critical role in playing out Disney's service standards. What is the purpose of the greeter?

- Greet the Guests (Courtesy)

- Answer questions they may have about the attraction (Safety, Courtesy, Efficiency)

- Handle individual needs, such as those with mobility challenges (Safety, Courtesy, Efficiency)

- Add to the overall show and theme of the experience (Show)

- Identify any Guests who do not meet certain ride requirements (Safety, Efficiency)

The Exterior of The Haunted Mansion – If you go back a few years ago, you'll recall that the Haunted Mansion had formal parterre gardens. Everything was meticulously landscaped, in keeping with Walt Disney's edict when the Haunted Mansion was originally built in Disneyland. Some of the original depictions of the Haunted Mansion in Disneyland suggested a broken down, weedy, and abandoned look. Walt saw the drawings and encouraged otherwise. "We'll take care of the outside and let the ghosts take care of the inside."[6]

But that doesn't necessarily work in Florida. First, while most Guests to Disneyland come from California, a much larger share of Guests visiting the Magic Kingdom come from other countries. Many of

---

[6] Jason Surrell, *The Haunted Mansion: From the Magic Kingdom to the Movies.* 1st ed. New York: Disney Editions.

them do not speak enough English to understand what the attraction title "Haunted Mansion" means. And there was little at the outset of the experience that would communicate what awaited you on the inside. Now, in part as a Courtesy and in part in the context of Show, the exterior of the Haunted Mansion is purposely poorly maintained. Added to it are other effects such as a Pet Cemetery, a horseless hearse, and thunder/lightning in the evening hours. It's all intended to communicate what the story and experience of the Haunted Mansion is going to be about.

Another element you wouldn't find at the Haunted Mansion in 1971 was a canopy over the queue. In California, the weather doesn't necessitate having one. In Florida, the rules are different. Orlando, in particular, is the lightening capital of the world. Indeed, as part of Safety and Courtesy, you will find a canopy or roof overhead just as you do in other attractions such as the indoor queue for Pirates of the Caribbean or the canopy over the Mad Tea Party. These are examples of operational decisions made utilizing the four service keys.

PRIORITIZED, OR FIRST AMONG PEERS

Some say that Disney's four keys are prioritized and that they go in the order shown. Others would say that they are peers, with Safety being first among peers. Here's what one Disney leader noted:

"This topic is near and dear to my heart, so while I'm always an observer to these discussions, this time I'd like to share an insight or two. The four keys are alive and well, and were the foundation for opening Hong Kong Disneyland. Coming from an operator who is responsible for the application of the four keys every day in our park, Safety is the first among peers. Anyone who has ever seen a Cast Member or a Guest injured and realized the impact it has on them, their families and the leaders responsible will understand why Safety has to be paramount in all that we do. Safety can't be encompassed in Efficiency. On a construction project, a worker was using a power washer to clean the floor. When he pulled the trigger of the wand, the power of the blast of the water was unexpected and he lost control of the wand. The water (with pressure equivalent to a sand blaster) fired straight into the face of a worker standing behind the first worker. The only thing that saved the eye of the second worker was the goggles he was wearing. The only reason he was wearing the goggles is because we had made it a site safety requirement (even though it wasn't legally required) earlier in the project. This is one of thousands of examples that could be used to explain why Safety must always be 'first among peers.'"

"Another point that may be interesting is (other than Safety), there is no priority among the four keys. ALL keys have to be accomplished simultaneously. We can't choose Show over Efficiency. We have to do both. Communicating (and demonstrating) that concept is a significant leadership challenge, but because it inherently creates "creative conflicts", we are pushed to do things and go places that would normally be perceived as too difficult, or too far. The unyielding nature of the four keys (and how they interact) is a powerful catalyst for continuous organizational renewal when it comes to how we think about excellence."

Whether you see them ranked or whether you see them as peers, it's important that you identify what they are to you and then use them as a decision making filter—either your priorities in order of 1, 2, 3 and so on, or your first priority, and then a focus on how to make all other priorities come alive as well. The importance thing is that there is dialogue and alignment throughout the organization.

Simple service standards can be powerful tools in any organization. And there is power in establishing a framework of values from which everyone operates. Within that framework, you can empower employees in a way that gives them a sense of ownership and purpose. You can create a consistent image across the entire organization. Disney's Four Keys have stood the test of time for over 40 years. You can create standards within your own organization that will stand the test of time as well.

We've looked at the strategy for putting a great Guest experience into place. In the next section that follows, we'll deliver that experience by incorporating these standards into everything we do in the organization.

Building Your Service Keys

Looking in your own Magic Mirror, ask yourself:

- Do I have standards or values that succinctly define the service I offer?

- Is each standard I've identified unique in what it offers as a service to others?

- Do I have the right number of standards to make my organization stand out, but not too many that they're difficult to remember?

- Do my standards encompass the work of the entire organization?

- Have I prioritized those standards? Is there at least one standard that stands out as a non-negotiable or a "first among peers"?

SECTION

II

THE HAND OF SERVICE

THE ACTIONS NEEDED TO BUILD
A STRONG SERVICE CULTURE

*"WE TRAIN THEM TO BE AWARE
THAT THEY'RE THERE MAINLY TO HELP THE GUEST."*

--WALT DISNEY

8

DISNEY'S SERVICE BEHAVIORS

ALIGNING BEHAVIORS TO VALUES

In the last couple of chapters we talked about Disney's approach to creating a great Guest experience. We've overviewed the service theme: "We Create Happiness" and Disney's Four Keys: "Safety, Courtesy, Show, and Efficiency." We've spoken about understanding what Guests really need and providing for that.

Moving forward, let's discuss the basic service behaviors expected of both Disney Cast Members and managers. These service behaviors:

- Define behavior in terms of how you interact with customers.

- Create a common baseline for interaction with customers.

- Demonstrate the elements of performance that perpetuate the standards—such as "courtesy."

- Communicate employee responsibilities and company expectations.

- Initiate customizing service to individual customers.

The typical tendency for leaders is to try and map out all of the possible behaviors their employees should demonstrate when working with customers. This approach is flawed for two important reasons. First, such behaviors tend to come across to the Guests as rote, rather than genuine. Second, it is impossible to map out all the potential behaviors individuals might demonstrate for future unforeseen circumstances. Attempting to compile such a comprehensive list is comparable to the common listing of dozens of rules for swimming at the local community pool. The list is usually so long that invariably no one pays attention at all—making the attempt a waste of time and effort.

TAKE 1: SEVEN SERVICE GUIDELINES

Let's look at what those service behaviors look like at Disney. For many years they have been known as Disney's Seven Service Guidelines. There were seven of them:

1. Make eye contact and smile.
2. Greet and welcome each and every Guest.
3. Seek out Guest contact.
4. Provide immediate service recovery.
5. Display appropriate body language.
6. Preserve the magical Guest experience.
7. Thank each and every Guest.

At one point they were re-scripted and tied to Disney's Snow White and the Seven Dwarfs:

1. Be *Happy*...make eye contact and smile!

2. Be like *Sneezy*...greet and welcome each and every Guest. Spread the spirit of Hospitality....It's contagious!

3. Don't be *Bashful*...seek out Guest contact!

4. Be like *Doc*....provide immediate Service recovery!

5. Don't be *Grumpy*...always display appropriate body language at all times!

6. Be like *Sleepy*...create DREAMS and preserve the "MAGICAL" Guest experience!

7. Don't be *Dopey*...thank each and every Guest!

The guidelines were posted in many places backstage, particularly in the areas right before you stepped on-stage. While they succeeded for many years, there were some challenges. "Make eye contact" and "Thank each and every Guest," communicated to the 18-year-old popcorn seller exactly how to follow the guidelines. Other behaviors were more vague, such as "Provide immediate service recovery" or "Display appropriate body language." You would need more specific behaviors to define to an eighteen year old what exactly he or she was supposed to do.

TAKE 2: DISNEY BASICS

Surveys conducted with thousands of Disney Guests and Cast Members eventually led to re-looking at the Seven Service Guidelines. In time, they created what was known as The Disney Basics. This new set of behaviors was broken down into two parts. The first set of guidelines focuses on all Cast Members and the second on management. Here are those dealing with Cast Members:

I project a positive image and energy.
- *Smile*
- Look approachable
- Look happy and interested
- Model the Disney Look
- Keep conversations positive

I am courteous and respectful to all Guests, including children.
- Make eye contact and smile
- Engage in Guest interaction
- Treat Guests as individuals
- Greet and welcome each Guest
- Thank all Guests and invite them back

I stay in character and play the part.
- Preserve and protect the magic
- Provide excellent show quality and safety
- Perform role efficiently by reducing hassles and inconveniences

I go above and beyond.
- Anticipate needs and offer assistance
- Create surprises and Magical Moments
- Provide immediate service recovery

What is ideal about this effort is that this list is collapsible: you can look at just the four headlines, or you can also identify key behaviors for each. Many of the earlier seven service behaviors fall within the new guidelines, and new ones emerge, such as "Treating Guests as individuals" or "Look happy and interested." These are ideas that could be transferable to any organization.

Also note each of these areas begins with the word "I" in front of each statement—suggesting that each Cast Member should take ownership in executing these guidelines.

TAKE 3: DISNEY'S FOUR SERVICE KEYS

The problem with The Service Basics is that they really didn't align with Disney's original Four Keys. Originally, the Basics had been aligned with the Four Keys. But the initial efforts proved too cumbersome and confusing. So they were rolled out without a direct reference to the Four Keys. They simply sat separately.

Simultaneously but separately in my own consulting, I saw the same thing as we worked with clients as varied as hospitals, government agencies, or trucking companies. We began creating behaviors that aligned with each of the core standards that were established. That way, there was a tiered effect for learning. A new employee going through an orientation might only remember the 4-5 keys or standards being shared, but in time they could learn the behaviors that go with them.

So it wasn't too surprising when we eventually heard that Disney had decided to go back the drawing board and re-align The Disney Basics to the Four Keys. They now have a tiered effect. The first tier consists of four keys or values. These are followed by 2-3 key practices for those standards. Then there are behaviors listed under each. Here are the keys, the actions, and their behaviors in their new form:

Safety

I practice safe behaviors in everything I do.

- Know and follow all safety policies and procedures.
- Safely deliver on Courtesy, Show and Efficiency.
- Be aware of surroundings and the hazards that may be present.

I take action to always put safety first.
- Identify, correct, and immediately report safety concerns.
- Avoid shortcuts that do not put safety first.
- Ask, "Is there a safer way?"

I speak up to ensure the safety of others.
- Demonstrate care for the safety of others.
- Appreciate and encourage the safety efforts of others.

Courtesy

I project a positive image and energy.
- Smile.
- Be approachable and make eye contact.

I am courteous and respectful to Guests of all ages.
- Greet, welcome, and thank all Guests.
- Engage in Guest interactions.
- Keep conversations positive and appropriate.
- Treat each Guest as an individual.

I go above and beyond to exceed Guest expectations.
- Create surprises and Magical Moments.
- Anticipate needs and offer assistance.
- Provide immediate service recovery.

Show

I stay in character and perform my role in the show.
- Use themed language and actions that support the story of my area.

- Preserve the magic.
- Model the Disney Look

I ensure my area is show-ready at all times.
- Keep areas clean and well maintained.
- Take action to correct or report distractions from the show.

Efficiency

I perform my role efficiently so Guests get the most out of their visit.
- Look for ways to reduce lines and hassles.
- Provide accurate and timely information.
- Be knowledgeable about my area and beyond.
- Share opportunities to improve my area.

I use my time and resources wisely.
- Be prepared and anticipate operational needs.
- Work as a team and build partnerships across all areas.
- Take responsibility to conserve resources.

Essentially, what has happened is that The Disney Basics have been largely evolved to the key points listed under Courtesy, with new actions and behaviors directed toward the other three keys. In another instance, research also showed that international partners mentioned the importance placed on showing attention toward seniors, and not just children, so the wording has been modified to "I am courteous and respectful to Guests of all ages."

The evolution Disney has made here has refocused energy around creating a great Guest experience. Moreover, this pattern is very helpful to organizations that want to create a great Guest service in their own organization, and I'll give some examples of this as well. The expression "simple but not simplistic" applies here. You keep to several key principles or values, but then you work very hard to implement those concepts every day in delivering great customer service.

There is one more important component to this list. Also identified in the Basics and in the Disney Keys behaviors are a list of leadership expectations. We will cover those in Section III.

Disney's Four Keys serve as a compass for creating happiness and serving others. More than fifty-five years later, these Four Keys serve as the foundation for everything Disney does. Any organization would be envious to have several key standards stand that test of time. It is at the heart of what has made Disney the powerful name it is today.

ESTABLISHING YOUR SERVICE BEHAVIORS

LOOKING IN YOUR OWN MAGIC MIRROR, ASK YOURSELF:

- WHAT ARE MY SERVICE BEHAVIORS OR GUIDELINES?

- HOW ARE THOSE BEHAVIORS CUSTOMIZED TO MY OWN ORGANIZATION?

- HOW CAN I ALIGN THOSE BEHAVIORS TO MY SERVICE STANDARDS?

- HOW CAN I MAKE OUR SERVICE BEHAVIORS COME ALIVE FOR OUR ORGANIZATION?

- HOW CAN I MAKE SUCH BEHAVIORS PART OF OUR CULTURAL DNA?

9

PROVIDING A GENUINE SMILE

Smile, darn ya, smile,
You know this whole world is a good world after all.
Smile, darn ya, smile,
And right away watch lady luck pay you a call.
Things are never black as they are painted,
Time for you and joy to get acquainted.
Make life worthwhile,
Come on and Smile, darn ya, smile.

SERVICE WITH A SMILE

You may remember this tune, which was re-popularized in the film, *Who Framed Roger Rabbit.* All of the 'toons come together at the end of the film and join in unison on these words.

The greatest symbol of traditional customer service is a smile. Having a smile is a part of what makes Disney legendary. In every version of Disney's service behaviors, smiling has been identified as a key component. It's been a heritage of Disney's to have their Hosts and Hostesses greet others with a smile.

All that said, it's not easy smiling at Walt Disney World. Sometimes it's hot out there. The humidity is high. Lightning storms are on their way. There are more Guests than one knows what to do with. Lines queue in every direction. Some Guests are frustrated, even angry; others are cheating in line or ruining the Guest experience for others. The other Cast Members are exhausted and tired. To make matters worse, the boss comes parading through from having been behind his desk in an air-conditioned office and reminds you to smile.

It's not easy—even at Disney. For instance, sometimes the prioritized standards of safety, courtesy, show, and efficiency lose their context. We spoke about everyone being pointed in one direction. But sometimes when the rubber hits the road, everything is not so magical. One Disney Cast Member put it this way:

"At my attraction we are constantly being pressured to be 'efficient.' They do ask us not to sacrifice courtesy over efficiency but at the end of the day all that matters are the counts each hour...with competitions between attractions to see who can accomplish the highest counts, sometimes we forget to slow down and give that simple smile you talk about. Yet if a Guest stops and asks me how my day is going, I always gladly stop my monotonous routine to talk to them and create a 'magical moment.'"

I find this response to be very authentic, and typical of how many people feel about being pleasant toward others. There are many benefits behind offering a smile.

WHY SMILE?

A large body of work has been done on why smiling matters. Indeed, a casual look on the Internet and you will find it is said that a genuine smile...

- Makes us more attractive.
- Helps us to change our mood.
- Provides us greater attention/notice from others around us.
- Boosts our immune system and overall health.
- Utilizes less facial/neck muscles--approximately 16 facial for smiling and some 43 for frowning.
- Lowers the blood pressure.
- Helps make people more successful in the long run.
- Helps us stay more positive.
- Releases endorphins that act as natural painkillers.
- Boosts levels of Serotonin, which regulates our moods, sleep,

sexuality, and appetite.

- Acts as a natural painkiller.
- Makes us look younger.
- Helps pave our mental attitude toward a better future.
- Releases a warmer vocal tone.
- Becomes contagious with others.
- Relieves our stress.
- Makes others more comfortable in our presence.
- Triggers certain hormones, lowering heart rates, and steadying breathing.
- Helps support our immune systems and fight illness.
- Helps us to live longer.
- Becomes contagious.
- Eases the tension in an embarrassing moment.

THE SECRET IS TO *SMILE*

If you want your employees to smile, then you need to think about what that takes. I have an acronym for this-S.M.I.L.E. SMILE isn't a "cute" glance. SMILE isn't some quick little rule-of-thumb for turning a frown upside down. Rather it represents what is foundational in an authentic display of courtesy. SMILE stands for the following:

S – Serve

It's about service. If you truly like serving others, a smile will be a natural extension of that attitude. Truth is, faking a smile is really about masking your attitude. If you have a lousy attitude, it's really hard to come across differently when communicating with others. And if your attitude is a conditional one, where you only act nice and smile to those who do the same, then you're going to deliver an inconsistent experience. Great customer service is unconditional service. Unconditional service requires having the best attitude possible no matter what. Having the best attitude requires keeping a smile on your face.

M – Mirror

If you want those around you to smile and be happy, you as a leader are going to have to authentically match that behavior. If you want fellow co-workers to smile, you have to lead the way. If you want the customer to be happy, you must take the initiative. You simply have to mirror the correct behaviors if you are going to expect it from others. It starts with a smile. And when you smile, try to match the emotional level others are at. If you are bouncing around like Bozo the Clown while someone is getting over his or her hangover via a morning cup of coffee, you'll lose the purpose behind the smile. That doesn't mean if they're grumpy, you be grumpy. But it does mean that smiling can simply be an act of pleasantry rather than an act of cheerleading.

I – "I Choose"

It's a choice to smile. The greatest power we as humans possess is our ability to choose. We are the only creatures in the animal kingdom who choose to smile. Dolphins may look smiley, but that look is fairly fixed. We, on the other hand, get to choose. And our smiles can't look like a fixed smile on a dolphin. You can't force someone to be pleasant with others. You can't make it part of their performance review. You don't get it by making others repeat cute and catchy phrases when they walk into your establishment. Even "Have a Magical Day" becomes less than magical if it's forced on every Cast Member's lips. By the way, some will say that you hire the smile and train the skill. Perhaps so, but whether smiling comes easy for you or not, you have to choose to smile with others. It's a choice.

L – Lighten Up

We could have also used L for Laughter. Keep a sense of humor. Bring it to the surface whenever possible. Try to keep things light— even when others are drawing you down. Given time and a little context, you will probably look back on some of your worse job experiences and have a good laugh. When it's hard to smile, find your laughing place and draw from it. For me, it's sharing my experience with my wife after a long day of work. But sometimes it's getting off the plane from a long gig and knowing I'm heading to a Disney park or the beach during the weekend. Find your "laughing place," and lighten up—especially when others aren't.

E – Engage

Employees who are not engaged in their work seldom keep a smile on their face for long. When I say engaged, what I mean is that they feel empowered, they feel a sense of ownership. They know what they're doing and what their role means to the mission of the organization. They have the tools and equipment to do their job. They receive feedback for doing a great job, as well as development in learning how to be even more effective. It's really difficult to expect employees to be happy and to genuinely demonstrate the emotion in their work if the work you give them is mundane and meaningless. You have to build employee engagement.

I see that engagement in all forms. On one occasion at Disneyland the Jungle Cruise skipper spent the time waiting for the dock to clear so he could pull in by asking the Guests where they were from. When one mentioned they were from Tucson, he took the time to introduce the desert-home Guests to water on the side of the boat. The day before, we engaged in a conversation with Oscar, a long-time Cast Member at Carnation Cafe. He has always been genuine and delightful and generous in his attention with us. Two days before, legendary Disneyland Cast Member Maynard hosted the introductory spiel at the Enchanted Tiki Room. His smile made a simple narrative event come alive.

Yet nothing caught our eye more than a Fantasyland Cast Member named Paula. Her job was to board and dispatch Guests on Peter Pan's Flight. She was so engaging that her smile and her countenance were striking. In a 10-15-second boarding experience she engaged all of Disney's Four Service Keys of Safety, Courtesy, Show, and Efficiency bringing them to life. She was a marvel to observe. I wondered if she was always this way. A year later, as my wife and I came back to Disneyland on a trip, there was Paula at the end of the

Snow White's Scary Adventures ride. She saw our anniversary badges and immediately went into a little tune celebrating our special occasion. Then she asked if we would like to stay on and ride the attraction again. When we came out of the ride a second time, she was managing a family with mobility challenges, all the while singing to us again and wishing us well. Her countenance was alive with a smile and a song! Clearly she demonstrates how much more enjoyable work can be when you are engaged in making your Guests happy.

Of course, if you're like W.C. Fields, you may be inclined to "start each day with a smile and get over it." After all, like my Gen-Y daughter says, some jobs are "super sucky," and even in the best job, there are days where you're not going to want to smile. Sometimes you have to acknowledge that the circumstances in which you find yourself are awful and uncomfortable. However, you still have to treat others—especially your fellow employees, with as much respect and dignity possible. Returning to the lyrics of our song, if you want to make life worthwhile, you have to learn to smile as often as possible-- even when you're not in it. After all, it's about attitude. And in the end, it's attitude that determines our fate. So, smile, make some magic in your own business, and...

Smile, darn ya, smile,
You know this whole world is a good world after all.
Smile, darn ya, smile,
And right away watch lady luck pay you a call.
Things are never black as they are painted,
Time for you and joy to get acquainted.
Make life worthwhile,
Come on and Smile, darn ya, smile.

PROVIDING A GENUINE SMILE

LOOKING IN YOUR OWN MAGIC MIRROR, ASK YOURSELF:

- DO I SMILE? DO I ENJOY SMILING? WHY? WHAT'S IN IT FOR ME?

- DO I FEEL AWKWARD SMILING? IF SO, HOW DO I MAKE IT PART OF MY OWN NATURE?

- CAN I FIND A SMILE IN SERVING OTHERS?

- DO I TAKE THE LEAD IN MODELING THE IMPORTANCE OF KEEPING A SMILE ON MY FACE?

- WHAT CAN I DO TO KEEP A SENSE OF HUMOR AND TO LIGHTEN UP?

- HOW DOES BEING ENGAGED KEEP ME FOCUSED ON OTHERS RATHER THAN ON MY OWN NEEDS? HOW CAN I STAY MORE ENGAGED AND FIND A SMILE IN SERVING OTHERS?

10

GREETING GUESTS

ASSERTIVE FRIENDLINESS

There's an expression that's been around at Disney for many years. It's called being "assertively friendly." What does that mean? No one questions that Disney has been known for years as being friendly, but *assertively* friendly?

At face value, one might be concerned that being assertively friendly means "in your face" courtesy. Of course, there's a problem with that. Such an approach can be received poorly at times, or even be perceived as "weird" at the very least. Too much of it, and suddenly Disney seems more "robotic." Neither of which would be appropriate, of course. So what does *assertive* mean in the Disney context?

I rather prefer thinking of assertive as being "proactive" or "forward-thinking." I asked my daughter, who is working through college, what assertive friendliness looked like, and she described the protocol required of employees at the counter service restaurant where she works. Every employee is required to greet his or her entering customers with a scripted, themed expression.

You've had this experience—it's common to many different shops and restaurants where they greet you with a rote expression. Some expressions are cute, others ordinary, but they all share one thing in common—they eventually become mundane and meaningless. And that's a big drawback. It becomes scripted after a while. Any excitement wears out when you're asked to do the exact same thing day in and day out. Then when the boredom sets in, as it always does, mischievous workers start utilizing other creative catch phrases to endure the mundane activity.

The same can be said of saying goodbye to customers. The first time I heard a Disney operator or reservationist say, "Have a Magical Day," I was completely impressed. Now, I know I'm not their target audience, I experience Disney far too closely than their targeted customer. But I can't help but think that there are more personal, more creative, more imaginative expressions than just "Have a Magical Day."

Disney has audio-animatronic figures that can give repetitive statements. Great employees are the ones who can observe, assess, and respond individually to the needs of others.

My business partner, Mark David Jones, and I worked with a global customer service organization where many of the international locations kept requesting "scripted" greetings as well as responses. "Just tell us what to say and we'll get them to say it." Some hotels have defined themselves over the years by providing certain scripted greetings, but little of that works well with customers in today's world. If anything—it's marginalizing the customer experience in the end.

The practice brings up an important question: Why do we even bother greeting or talking to customers? The answer is that we want to build customer loyalty through great Guest experiences. We want our Guests to continue visiting our business and utilizing our products and services. We want them to be advocates in getting others to use our products and services. How do we do this? We do this through creating relationships and providing service that meets—or better yet—exceeds their expectations.

GREETING GUESTS AT RADIATOR SPRINGS

Now let's suppose we're Cast Members at the Curio Shop in Radiator Springs at Disney California Adventure. Guests come in and out throughout the day. Part of being courteous requires we greet Guests as they come into our shop. How do we start a conversation? There are several ways, and all of them can succeed if applied appropriately. Let's look at each:

1. Open-ended questions – These are great because they provide wider opportunities for understanding your Guests. The following are examples of open-ended questions you may want to ask those you meet:

- What other parks or attractions have you visited?
- What Disney character friends do you most enjoy visiting when you come here?
- How are you planning on spending your time today?

Open-ended questions are the fastest way to gain better understanding of your customers. Understanding our customers is critical if you are to provide great, tailored service that exceeds expectations, but there are other ways to jump-start a conversation.

2. Closed-Ended Questions –The next are closed-ended questions. Here are some examples:

- Where are you from?
- Have you been on Radiator Springs Racers yet?
- Do you collect or trade pins?

Closed-ended questions are often those that are answered with a short response, or a "yes" or "no." There is nothing wrong with this. It can be a good starting place if it helps you clarify their needs, but they are best used when there is an open-ended question following. Alone, they are not very useful, unless the Guest takes the question and elaborates. For instance, asking, "How are you?" is typically going to foster the response "Fine." Where do you go from there? While that may break the ice, it doesn't go anywhere. You want to ask closed-ended questions that can help you go somewhere. In other words, you want to think through where you want to go with a response that will take you to a better place. For example:

"Is this your first time at the park?"

> If so – "What do you think? How are you enjoying your time?
> If not – "What are your favorite attractions when you visit?"

3. Finding Something in Common – Finding something in common makes conversation much easier to direct. Clothing, accessories, articles of possession, hometowns, and even shared names are places where people find something in common.

- "From your cap and T-shirt I can tell you're a big Lakers fan. Did you see last Friday's game?"
- "You have twins. My sister has twins as well. What are their ages?"

4. Directing Their Attention – Focusing your conversation toward something other than the two of you is another way to create conversation. A character making appearances in the park, a particular store item, or simply flowers in bloom can be a great way to direct the conversation and get it started. What are some examples of directing their attention?

- "I like the Tinker Bell shirt you have on. We just got a new set of Tinker Bell and her friends."
- "I see you're newlyweds. Congratulations, did you get honorary buttons for each of you to wear?"

5. Offering Compliments – Complimenting an individual or members of their party makes for a great opportunity to build relationships, but make sure the compliment is specific and genuine. Let's look at some examples:

- "That looks like a great stroller. Does it fold up easily?"
- "That's an awesome hairstyle. Is it easy to keep up?"
- "So, you're a veteran? Thank you for your service. In which branch did you serve?"

6. Talking Weather - Discussing the weather is an often-used topic, but it's disarming and gets the customer talking about something where anyone can be the expert. It can provide an opportunity to use the topic as a transition to better meeting their needs. What are some examples of discussing the weather?

- "Your jacket looks like it's keeping you warm on a cold night like this. Where did you buy it?"
- "Well, at least now you're out of the heat! What brings you in aside from the hot weather?"

In summary, small talk and simple questions serve an important purpose when they help us to build relationships and deliver exemplary service.

DON'TS AND DOS

What are some don'ts and dos about initiating conversations?

Let's start with the things you *shouldn't* do:

- Don't talk only about yourself.
- Don't say anything that sounds scripted or canned.
- Don't drill the Guest with questions. The intent is not to know everything about the person, or even to keep the conversation going as long as possible. The purpose is to build relationships, find opportunities to provide service.
- Don't invade their personal space. Be especially aware of this when it comes to dealing with other cultures.
- Don't bring up topics that are too controversial or political.

Here are some *should* dos:

- Provide eye contact.
- Smile.
- Listen.
- Acknowledge immediately.
- Keep up and refer to current events.
- Use their name whenever available or known.
- Individualize whenever possible.
- Find subjects they may know something about.
- Get on the same level with smaller children.
- Most important, learn something about them so that you can

better serve them.

GREETING INSIDE AND OUT

Greeting your customers seems like such a basic thing—indeed it sounds like an *obvious* thing to do. But how often do we fail to do it? I rather like the approach Ritz-Carlton takes. The expectation among the "ladies and gentlemen serving ladies and gentlemen" is that no employee should pass by another Guest OR another employee without greeting the individual in passing.

What a great expectation! *Greet customers!* No wonder they're respected for their exemplary service. More importantly, is that the expectation is made of each other as employees. Talk about a no-cost method for dramatically changing the culture. Imagine if you could just do one thing—ask your employees to greet one another. Simply ask them to say "Hi" or another short greeting of some kind—we don't want rote behavior here, remember. In doing so, you'll not only improve morale, you'll create habits that are then automatically shared with Guests and customers.

GREETING YOUR CUSTOMERS

LOOKING IN YOUR OWN MAGIC MIRROR, ASK YOURSELF:

- WHAT EXPECTATIONS DO I HAVE ABOUT GREETING CUSTOMERS?

- WHEN I GREET SOMEONE, IS IT SINCERE AND INDIVIDUALIZED?

- HOW DO I APPROACH GREETING OTHERS?

- WHAT ARE THE WAYS I COULD IMPROVE MY GREETING OF OTHERS?

- IS GREETING AN INTERNAL CUSTOMER AS IMPORTANT TO ME AS GREETING AN EXTERNAL CUSTOMER?

11

MAKING GUESTS FEEL MAGICAL

TRANSACTIONS VS. INTERACTIONS

Disney knows that over a typical resort stay, on average, Guests will have over 60 moments of contact with Cast Members. Those moments mean nothing if they are simply *transactions*. It could mean everything if any of them are *interactions*. Consequently, Disney has a vested interest in providing as many opportunities as possible for Cast Members to make each individual Guest experience special. The idea and practice of Cast Members doing something special for the Guests they serve has been going on for years. But in the 1990s, this took on a greater structure at Walt Disney World. That structure would become known as "Magical Moments" and "Take 5s."

In a previous chapter on smiling I spoke of Disney Cast Members like Oscar, Maynard and Paula, who have mastered the art of interacting. Paula, especially, was expert in taking a very routine duty, like boarding Guests onto a ship in Peter Pan's Flight, while creating an interaction that was memorable, but kept the operation as running efficiently as ever. It's important to take time for your Guests, but you'd be surprised how little time it takes to make that special moment. It's especially seen among my Cast Member friends and colleagues who, even when off duty, still come up to people in Orlando who are taking a photo, and offer to take the picture so both can be in it.

What are Magical Moments and Take 5s? Who else does something like this? Providing Magical Moments and Take 5s:

- Are critical to creating customer loyalty.

- Help to engage employees.

- Can be a high touch support to high tech offerings.

- Help in providing great service recovery.

- Succeed when you give employees the permission to freely do so.

- Are contagious when they happen!

Let's look at each and understand what they look like.

MAGICAL MOMENTS

Magical Moments are carefully orchestrated opportunities to individualize the customer experience. Magical Moments are planned, scheduled events that create special moments for the Guest.

Have you ever been chosen to be the grand marshal of the 3:00 parade? By pulling the Sword out of the Stone in Fantasyland, have you ever been made the temporary king or queen of England by Merlin? As a veteran were you selected as a Guest of honor for the evening flag retreat? Did the elevator open at The Tower of Terror only to see your child dressed as a bellhop?

What's this—children dressed as bellhops? Yep! There have been all sorts of opportunities created as Magical Moments. From time to time, youngsters too short to actually ride The Tower have been afforded an opportunity to dress up as a bellhop at Disney's Hollywood Studios and greet their family coming off of the elevator.

Magical Moments show up in all sorts of places. This includes:

- Guest of the day programs
- Honorary titles, badges, buttons, and certificates
- Honorary roles in shows, demonstrations, or attractions
- Hands-on activities unique to the location
- Special games and activities for the children

Here's an account from my friends, David and Leah Zanolla, of an experience they had when they took their son on a special birthday trip:

> "We surprised our son Jonah with a trip to Walt Disney World for his 4th birthday. His brother and sister weren't coming along; it was just him, Mommy and Daddy. We were obviously a bit worried he'd miss his siblings, so we were trying to make it a special trip. We arrived the night before his birthday and, even though it was well past his bedtime, we went to the Magic Kingdom for a couple of hours. On our way in, we got his birthday button in preparation for the next day. Then, we headed over to the Chapeau on Main Street to get him a pair of mouse ears to help him celebrate.
>
> Upon entering the shop, Jonah found two pairs of hats between which he was having troubling choosing. One was a very "loud" hat that read 'Happy Birthday.' The other had ears that lit up with fireworks. He liked this one as well, because he's a kid and fireworks are cooler than mom and dad. While he was making what appeared to be a life-altering decision about the hats, a Cast Member walked over, knelt down and started a conversation with him.
>
> "Jonah, is it your birthday?" she asked.
>
> "Tomorrow," he replied in a little kid's voice absent of proper 'R' sounds.
>
> "Guess what?" she said. "Mickey would like to buy you a hat for you to wear on your birthday tomorrow! You pick out which one you want and bring it to me. He even asked us to put your name on the back."
>
> Jonah was thrilled. His face lit up as he looked at us. This Cast Member didn't offer to buy his hat—Mickey did. He ended up picking out the fireworks hat and we left the store with a beaming almost-4-year-old...and a beaming hat.

Since I know how important Cast Member recognition is to the culture of Walt Disney World, I knew we needed to make sure this Cast Member got a pat on the back for making my son's day. We headed over to City Hall to visit Guest Relations. When it was our turn, Paul from Baltimore greeted us at the counter. We explained to Paul what a Magical Moment had been created in the Chapeau and asked if we could fill out a comment card for that Cast Member. He intently listened to our story and promised us he would make sure she was recognized, but he didn't stop there.

He leaned over the counter and asked Jonah when his birthday was. When Jonah told him it was tomorrow, he asked if he'd be visiting the Magic Kingdom on his birthday. A frequent visitor to the parks, Jonah responded that yes, he'd be there early because "there were Extra Magic Hours." Paul then asked us if we could bring Jonah back to City Hall the next morning and tell them Paul had left something for him.

The next morning, as promised, we were in the first wave of Guests into the Magic Kingdom. We headed straight to City Hall and we quietly delivered the message as Paul requested. The Cast Member with whom we were speaking came back with a large bag with a note that said, "Hope you have a magical birthday." It was signed, "Your Friend, Paul." Inside the bag was a large plush Mickey Mouse that brought an even larger smile to Jonah's face. The results? Two Magical Moments. Two amazing Cast Members going above and beyond. One happy 4-year-old."

Now as a caveat—please don't go into the Chapeau on Main Street expecting a free hat as you announce your birthday. Nor should you expect something similar from City Hall. It doesn't work that way. It's a timing thing, determined by many, many factors. What's important to understand is that the individual Cast Members had the liberty to act on that opportunity at their discretion. And they were given the resources to make it happen. While this is not a frequent "once-every-hour" kind of experience, it's by no means infrequent as well. Still, it's very magical when it happens.

TAKE 5S

Hundreds of thousands have had some experience in a structured magical moment. But hundreds of thousands isn't enough. Disney needs *millions* of Guests to have a magical experience. That's where Take 5s come into play. Take 5s are "in the moment" opportunities Cast Members have to offer special Guest moments. Take 5s give license to the staff to take just 5 minutes out of their day to individualize customer service. If thousands of Cast Members can take 5 minutes a day to really pay attention to a customer, the results can be enormous.

Take 5s can be proactive or reactive. From a proactive perspective, it can take the form of going out and greeting Guests and looking for opportunities to be helpful. From a reactive view, it can be as simple as offering to take a picture of a customer who's already struggling with a photo opportunity. Simply put, Take 5s are a chance to do something nice for someone else in need.

What's wonderful about Take 5s is that they empower Cast Members to go out of their way to create happiness for the Guests. The genuineness of doing so is what makes Take 5s succeed. It may be replacing a spilled ice cream for a small child. It may be a housekeeper leaving a child's plush Mickey on the bed with a remote in hand watching the Disney Channel. It could be the entire boat singing happy birthday to you on board the Jungle Cruise, or Slue Foot Sue doting over your receding hairline.

Here is one instance that was re-told to me by a colleague of mine, Ty Lagerberg when he worked a few years ago in security at Disney. It started as a Magical Moment that became a Take 5 and even then some. It began as another "Make a Wish" experience. The little seven year old girl's final wish was to visit her favorite princess, Cinderella. As usual, arrangements had been made for the child and her family to be flown out to Orlando, Florida to visit the parks. But by the time the family arrived in Orlando, she was too weak to even go to the hotel and her family took her directly to the hospital. She would not be able to go to the castle to see Cinderella. But Cinderella might just come to her.

To Ty, it was another evening shift for the dispatchers at the Security Communications Center when he got the phone call at 10:30 that a nurse at the hospital had called about a very sick little girl there who so wanted to see Cinderella and could we help make that dream come true. That wasn't in anyone's job description. And it wasn't in the schedule. But word came through of the need, and the entire team sprang into action. Ty called the Character Zoo at the Magic Kingdom and found out that Cinderella had just finished the Main Street Electrical Parade and was still changing in her dressing room. Her manager asked Cinderella if she would be willing to delay her departure for a couple hours and make a special visit. Cinderella was more than happy to put her dress back on and provide some very special magic for one of her admirers. So less than an hour before midnight, Cinderella, her chaperone, and a security host departed for the 23-mile trip to the hospital. The company vehicle was no pumpkin coach, but then again it was going where no pumpkin coach typically went.

So ironic, when Cinderella arrived at the hospital--it was nearly midnight. The tiny patient had greatly faded, but her eyes lit up when the iconic princess entered the room. So beautiful and striking was she dressed in soft royal hues--that the rest of the team simply stepped to the side unnoticed. They knew the real world of the parks, the daily grind, the on-going bureaucracy. They knew Cinderella as much in plain clothes as in a ballroom dress. But they knew this would be no ordinary visit.

Cinderella called the girl by name, hugged the child, and sitting at her bedside softly conversed with her. Parents looking on could hardly contain themselves emotionally, and everyone was swallowing hard as well. But Cinderella stayed focused on the child. After all, she was Cinderella. When the little girl was too weak to converse, Cinderella picked up a book, read stories, and gave her an autographed photo of all the Disney Princesses. That would go on for over an hour, until the little girl finally went to sleep. Then as quietly as she came, Cinderella and her team departed leaving her little subject with the memories of a dream come true.

It wasn't until 6:30 the next morning that Ty and his security team realized how special that one dream come true really. Another call came to the Security Communications Center from the nurse at the hospital thanking Cinderella and the whole team for providing one little princess her final wish. She had passed away in her sleep shortly after 6 AM dreaming of her special royal visit.

Perhaps in the daily work grind none of us are princes or princesses — but we certainly have the opportunity to be heroes and heroines. It may not be in your job description. But these are the opportunities to create Magic.

So, how do you make that kind of thing happen in your own organization? After all, you don't have castles and safaris in our office. Well, magical moments and memories can happen. In fact, they've been happening since you were a small child. Remember when you went to the dentist as a child? If you were good, you could have something from the treasure chest. Have you been unexpectedly upgraded to a better car at the rental office, without paying more? What about a nurse who really looked after you and went the extra mile while you were in the hospital? Is there a hairdresser you continually return to because he or she fusses over you? Those memories are all the result of Take 5s.

Wish your organization were as magical as Disney? Remember, it isn't the pixie dust. It's the service you render.

MAKING YOUR CUSTOMERS FEEL MAGICAL

LOOKING IN YOUR OWN MAGIC MIRROR, ASK YOURSELF:

- ARE THERE MAGICAL MOMENTS (ONGOING, STRUCTURED EVENTS) OR TAKE 5S (IN-THE-MOMENT OPPORTUNITIES) I CURRENTLY PROVIDE?

- HOW CAN I MAKE THESE INTERACTIVE AND ENGAGING, RATHER THAN TRANSACTIONAL AND ROTE?

- HOW CAN I DO THIS INTERNALLY AS WELL AS EXTERNALLY?

- HOW CAN I REMEMBER TO DO THIS DAILY SO THAT WE ARE CONSTANTLY CREATING WONDERFUL EXPERIENCES FOR OUR CUSTOMERS?

12

FRONT OF THE HOUSE--BACK OF THE HOUSE

IS THERE REALLY A SECRET TUNNEL?

One of the most-requested activities by our program participants is an opportunity to visit the infamous "tunnel" underneath the Magic Kingdom. Of course, to most of our readers who know that you can't build underground in a swamp, it's known by its more correct name, the "Utilidor."

I don't blame anyone who is curious about visiting. I had seen images and heard stories about it ever since my parents purchased a copy of Christopher Finch's *The Art of Walt Disney* back in the 1970s as a Christmas present for me. I must admit that my first act as a new Walt Disney World hire was to go and get parking stickers for the Magic Kingdom. I then immediately headed from there to the Utilidor to check it all out. Seeing the tunnel was No. 1 on my list of things to do as a new Cast Member.

By the time I actually arrived at the Utilidor, I had some 20 years to anticipate the experience since the Christmas morning I received that book. I'm not sure it lived up to the expectations I had, but I don't think any experience can match 20 years of expectations. Besides, I think I was more anxious that someone would ask what I was doing there. No one ever did, but to make it seem like I was "on business" I just kept walking. And walking. And walking. The Utilidor is extensive and it's not too difficult to simply get lost or turned around.

That said, for many it is quite blasé. Frankly, it's just a notch above hanging out in any typical service corridor. But between the long walkways of walls and pipes and tubes are reminders that you're not in just any location; you are indeed in the Magic Kingdom.

Since then, I have seen so many different backstage locations. Because of my unique role in bringing Disney Institute participants to a wide variety of benchmarking locations, I had many opportunities to see the breadth and scope of Walt Disney World—both onstage and backstage. I've been in laundries and waste water treatment plants. I've been underwater at The Living Seas and on the very top of the roof at The Twilight Zone Tower of Terror. Through it all, I've learned some important lessons about separating the front of the house from the back of the house.

SEPARATE ONSTAGE FROM THE BACKSTAGE

Here's an example of how important it is at Disney that the front of the house be separated from the back of the house. There is a simple but fascinating place backstage that Guests onstage seldom see. As performers step out to perform in the parade at the Magic Kingdom, there's a line painted on the asphalt just before it intersects with Splash Mountain. If you look carefully, as you head into Frontierland on the Walt Disney World Railroad just prior to entering the tunnel of Splash Mountain, you can see the line for yourself. That line represents the line of sight for Guests "onstage". Before that line, behavior is strictly "backstage." But cross that line and you're in character and you *stay* in character. If you're Mickey, you're Mickey until you cross that line. If you're a dancer, you dance from that line until you cross a similar line backstage behind City Hall. It's amazing how they endure being in character until they cross that line. Stepping over the line at the end of the parade, you are greeted by backstage Cast Members who quickly bring you something to drink and help those in heavy costumes get out quickly. All of this teamwork is to help make sure that the experience is as magical at the end of the parade route as it is at the beginning. It all creates a tremendous emotional event for Guests if you separate what is onstage from what is backstage.

Having shared the context by which I have come to know Walt Disney World, let me say that I have learned some important insights about separating the back of the house experience from the front of the house experience. The same applies to what happens to an operation after hours, as well as what is seen by the customer before construction is completed. These insights can help many organizations to improve the service they deliver.

Let me share the important lessons in separating the front of the house from the back of the house:

PRESERVE THE GUEST EXPERIENCE

When Disneyland was created, there was no Utilidor. In fact, it was very difficult to access each land from the backstage area. The result was that Jungle Cruise skippers were going from the dressing area behind Tomorrowland, cutting across Main Street, and then going into their area of operation. All of this out of context activity seemed to ruin the themed experience.

So when Walt Disney World was created, they decided that they could best preserve the Guest experience by letting Cast Members cross under the park through the Utilidor.

Likewise, there is a great deal of activity that needs to happen in preparation of hosting guests at the park. For instance, pallets of merchandise must be moved to stores in Adventureland, Frontierland, and Liberty Square. So much product, in fact, that it can't be brought in just overnight. Those stores sit in the middle of the park. The only way you can access these stores are through the themed areas of the park or from underneath, so building a Utilidor system made sense.

The problem was, building a Utilidor was an expensive idea. Therefore, when Epcot was built, the Utilidor concept was very limited to supporting functions in the "Communicore" area of the park. Yes, there is a Utilidor at Epcot, however it's not well utilized. Rather, much of what happens backstage occurs around the perimeter of Epcot. Because of the distance involved, buses take Cast Members from one location to another.

Disney's Animal Kingdom utilizes the same peripheral approach design, but without a utilidor-style feature. Disney's Hollywood Studios is a different story. The idea there is to replicate an actual Hollywood studio, seeing people walking in a Star Tours outfit in front of an Indiana Jones Adventure is supposed to make the experience more authentic. That said, there are places the Guests never see, especially among those are locker and dining locations for Cast Members to get a respite from the Guests.

This is not about utilidors, or the lack thereof. It is about Disney's commitment to preserve the Guest experience. Since immersive theming is a big part of the show, it's important that you separate onstage from backstage. What is it that you don't want your customers to see? What price will you pay to preserve that Guest experience?

GIVE ME A BREAK

Let's face it, any employee needs space away from customers—and that's no less true at Walt Disney World. Such a facility needs to be away from the customers, so that employees can "let their hair down." Traditionally, that means an outdoor and an indoor location. Often those who work outdoors want to take a break inside, and those who are inside all of the time want to get out into the sunshine.

I mention this because of what people observe when they go to some gas station or even a big box store. In many, if not most locations, you find a break area right in front of the store where customers cross by to enter. They sit there smoking, eating, or simply chatting. Guests shouldn't be greeted in that way. They don't pretend that employees don't need a break, they just find it peculiar that they don't place that location somewhere where the employees aren't in line of sight of the customers. At any rate, it's hard to believe it's much of a break for them either to have everyone passing by them.

For that matter, any time you see an employee standing in front of a store or place of business smoking a cigarette or talking on a cell phone, you have created a poor image of what your operation is all about. It's a poor first impression and is often what contributes to the clutter and litter found in front of the store. You would never imagine seeing Cinderella out in front of the park smoking a cigarette. Why is it much different with any employee.

By the way, not all employees work in a "customer" location. Some, like call center reps, are on the phone with customers. For some, the customers they serve may be internal rather than external. But they need a break as well. They need a time and place to go and "vent" or let off some steam or simply get away. This typically requires providing them that time and physical space apart. I've also noticed that many times, employees working inside, want to step outside; and those outside often want to seek refuge indoors during their break.

HEART OF THE HOUSE

Much of Disney backstage is really a lot like any organization—it's a business filled with offices and cubicles, computers and files. Offices can be found tucked in all over the property. Initially, my first desk was upstairs at the palace in Italy at Epcot. Later it was a few blocks from Sea World, way outside of the Disney property.

There is little space that hasn't been utilized as an office space backstage at Walt Disney World. When they can't find office space, you'll find it either in the form of mobile units or even formal office buildings like the SunTrust building or Team Disney building. When a nearby mall went under years ago, Disney purchased it and created office space out of it.

When Walt built his studio for his animators, he created the best environment possible. But when it came to the parks, he didn't want to spend money on offices, since he not only emphasized--but also modeled--the importance of being out among the Guests. Still, there is a need for the business of the operation to be handled. But that business should be kept largely away from the customer if it isn't necessary to the Guest experience.

The same is true of a myriad of back-of-the-house operations that Guests seldom see. There are laundries, power plants, warehouses, recycling centers, nurseries and workshops. Tens of thousands are employed in making the magic come alive—even though they themselves are seldom, if ever, seen by the Guest. We call these operations the "heart" of the house, because they affect so much of what ultimately happens onstage.

The trick is connecting your heart-of-the-house employees to what is happening with the Guest. One woman I knew was hired to be a pyro technician for Wishes. On one of her first nights of work, she was taken the front of Cinderella Castle to watch the show. Only they didn't direct her to watch the show. Rather, they instructed her to watch the Guests as they watched the show. The power of this show on the Guests made a deep impression on her. It was one that stayed riveted in her mind night after night when she was far away from them carefully launching off fireworks.

ENGINEER THE EXPERIENCE

Just like any show, you must have some kind of stage management. In the early days of the Magic Kingdom, that took the form of DACS (Digital Animation Control System). Now known as Engineering Central, it's a centralized location roughly underneath Peter Pan's Flight from where parades, attraction, music, lighting, and so forth can be managed. The same concept has been employed since the opening of Epcot. You may remember the Astuter Computer Revue by Sperry, which allowed Guests to see how Disney ran the entire Epcot operation. Since then, computers have become much smaller and decentralized. But the idea was to have systems in place to make sure that the Guest experience was consistently and successfully executed.

What many don't know is that Walt Disney World, for many years, has run a command center in the event of hurricanes or other major catastrophes. Located in a plain facility dedicated largely to telecommunications, this room looks more like a war room prepared for nuclear annihilation. From here, the leadership of the organization can run the operation of the entire resort, while monitoring incoming storms and maintaining contact with the outside world. For the few who visit this location, it's an incredible wow as to the kind of preparation Disney puts into safety. The message is this: Disney makes whatever investment necessary to engineer the very best Guest experience possible. Make sure that your facilities, even those backstage, are designed to engineer the best guest experience possible.

TESTING THE GUEST EXPERIENCE

Backstage areas offer places where you can test the Guest experience onstage without letting the general public see it. Here are some examples:

When the highly stylized look of The Walt Disney World Swan and Dolphin was being designed, planners were concerned about what the large tropical motif would look like in the bright Florida sun. Therefore, they painted a sample of what that would look like on the back of show buildings at Epcot. For years after the hotels were opened, you would see these leftover renderings standing 40-50 feet high.

Step backstage by the parade building at the Magic Kingdom and you see a wide array of paving stones and concrete finishings. Some look themed to Main Street, while others look themed to Tomorrowland and Adventureland. Having a location away from the Guests to test the look and feel of these walkways helps designers to make right choices in creating the finished product.

Likewise, step inside the Cast Services building at Epcot and you will find a strange assortment of carpets. Many textile retailers promise carpeting with lifetime warranties. Whether they live up to it is determined here, where Cast Members can walk over it day in and day out. It tells the operations team which carpets will take the kind of wear inflicted by millions of Guests.

One of the most unique places to test the Guest experience was behind Disney's Caribbean Beach resort in the 1990s. During these busy years of creating new Disney hotels, complete room mockups were created to allow designers to completely visualize the Guest experience. Everything, down to the linen and the towels were laid out in these rooms. Stories are even told of executives, including Michael Eisner, who would stay the night in these rooms to test them out. Part of the back-of-the-house experience is to prepare for the front-of-the-house experience.

THE THIRD SHIFT

Originally, part of Cinderella Castle was designed to be a possible apartment for Roy Disney, but he died before such could be created. Then it served as a location for phone operators when Guests dialed Walt Disney World. It was very close to becoming an apartment again during the 25th anniversary. The plans for placing an apartment or Guest suite in Cinderella Castle have been on the books for many years. The stumbling block was often the fact that the park is not a quiet, sweet haven at night. It's busy. There are trucks in the street. There are men and women hosing walkways or mowing lawns. There is construction that only happens at night. The decision to finally let someone stay the night in the castle still required someone acting as a concierge and not letting visitors wander out and about. It also requires limiting the Guest view when they are in the suite. The same requirement is made in the Disneyland suite above Pirates of the Caribbean where a concierge is required to stay the night in an adjacent office.

There is much that happens between closing and opening hours. Let me share one of my favorite memories. The night before the 25th Walt Disney World anniversary rededication, I came in with a film crew to shoot preparations for the event. At 3 a.m., I stood with a camera operator shooting the rehearsal for the re-enactment parade that was to follow the next morning. Main Street U.S.A. was lit up and we were the only ones on the sidewalk watching the rehearsal for the rededication. This rehearsal included a huge marching band, and more Disney characters than I have ever seen in one setting. Besides the director, they performed in front of my camera operator and me, and no one else. For me, it was magical and a moment I will not soon forget.

Such moments occur all the time, though most involve maintenance and construction work. Much is done to ready the show, and that activity is carried out at night when Guests are not around—or at least when they are asleep in the castle.

After all is said and done, the bottom line is: You can't rehearse with the Guests in the park or customers in your store. You have to provide a time where the park is readied for the next day or for a special upcoming event. Also, some of the most important work is done by those in the third shift. Disney doesn't call it the midnight shift—that often has a negative connotation with it. But they do many things to focus attention and recognition on those who are part of their third shift.

SUMMARY

In optimizing your organization, what is considered "public" in your business? What is considered "behind the scenes"? How do you separate these areas?

What activities need to be done in public, but should be carried out before or after the customers or others have arrived?

There are areas/activities your customers should never see. They may be:

- Areas unsafe or dangerous to them.

- Areas that do not pertain to the customer experience.

- Certain operational activities.

- Discussions that should not be held in front of the customers.

- Areas that permit employees time away from the customers and complaints to "let their hair down."

Remember that the back of the house should support the front of the house in delivering great service to the customer. Every part of the operation is important to the entire experience. And that is what helps create the magic in *your* business.

WORKING THE BACK OF YOUR OPERATION

LOOKING IN YOUR OWN MAGIC MIRROR, ASK YOURSELF:

- WHAT IS FRONT OF THE HOUSE IN MY OPERATION? WHAT AREAS DO MY CUSTOMERS SEE?

- WHAT IS BACK OF THE HOUSE? HOW DO THEY SUPPORT THE GUEST EXPERIENCE?

- WHAT AREAS OF THE OPERATION DO I NOT WANT MY GUESTS TO SEE?

- HOW DO I SEPARATE THE FRONT OF THE HOUSE FROM THE BACK OF THE HOUSE?

- WHAT BEHAVIORS SHOULD AND SHOULD NOT OCCUR IN FRONT OF CUSTOMERS?

- WHAT HAPPENS BACK OF THE HOUSE THAT SUPPORTS THE GUEST EXPERIENCE IN THE FRONT OF THE HOUSE?

- HOW DO WE SUPPORT, HONOR, AND RECOGNIZE THOSE ON A THIRD SHIFT WHO SUPPORT THE OPERATION AFTER HOURS?

13

WAYFINDING AT DISNEY

ARE WE THERE YET?

Are we there yet?" "Are we lost?" "Where's the bathroom?" "I have a question..."

Statements you hear at Disney hundreds of times a day. These questions are at the heart of "wayfinding." Wayfinding is often used to refer to traditional navigation methods used by people to get from here to there. In more modern times, wayfinding is used in the context of architecture to refer to the customer's experience of orientation and choosing a path within a constructed environment. It also refers to those architectural and design elements that aid a customer's orientation.

Though others do it well, Disney is one of the great benchmarks for wayfinding. Disney was doing this kind of thing long before the word wayfinding became popular. In fact, Disney has referred to it as part of what they call "Guestology." Through such studies, Disney not only uses strategic wayfinding devices to help people find their way, but to *direct* the Guest in the way Disney wants them go. Such lessons in wayfinding could benefit any variety of businesses:

- Mass transportation centers – bus, train, airport, and subway stations
- Meeting/gathering centers – convention centers, hotels, and office buildings
- Retail – stores, malls, payment centers, and restaurants
- Entertainment – parks, theaters, museums, stadiums, and multiplexes

- Recreational – parks, zoos, theme parks, beaches, gyms, and health clubs
- Public – schools, universities, government buildings, neighborhoods, and hospitals
- Streets – roads, highways, parking lots, and garages

The means through which we find our way varies. From pocket compasses to GPS, there are many ways to find where you are going:

- Architecture—Nothing is more obvious than being able to see the thing you are looking for
- Directional signage – labels, ceiling signage, billboards, and sandwich boards
- Announcements – verbal instructions and guidance
- Maps – guide maps and GPS systems
- Informational centers – building directories, kiosks, Web sites, and phone trees
- Layout – layout and color of pathways, entry ways, exits, and landscaping
- Employees—offering directions and guidance

LESSONS IN WAYFINDING

From "Which aisle has the hummus?" to "Where is gate C54?" we all depend on wayfinding techniques to get us where we need and want to be. Disney has a lot of experience on how to make wayfinding more successful. Consider the following examples:

Create a Simple Flow – Note the radial/wheel and spoke design of the original Disneyland park. While all Guests enter and exit through the same experience of walking down Main Street, U.S.A., the rest of the park allows the Guest to bisect through the park in a straight line, or by traveling in a broad circle around the perimeter of the park. You don't have to re-trace your steps to see the entire park. But you also don't have to walk the entire length of the park, if you want to get from point A to point B. All of the "Magic Kingdom" style parks throughout the world follow this same format.

At Epcot, you experience a sort of figure-8 design of Epcot that allows a perimeter stroll. Starting from Spaceship Earth, most Guests can work their way around the park, without having to re-trace their steps. Moving from point A to Point B however is a little trickier. In Future World you can bisect directly from one point to another. You can also take a Friendship boat to move in certain directions in World Showcase. But trying to move from Norway to Morocco is a walk-around. And moving from Future World to World Showcase and/or back again requires funneling through a corridor. There's no substitute for a well laid-out facility. Still, the design allows for a fairly natural flow of your experience.

Unfortunately, those same principles of flow did not occur at what was originally known as the Disney-MGM Studios. That park was originally laid out in a functional manner—with half of the park being dedicated to the Guests, but the other, and larger half, being laid out for the flow of a working studio. The Guest experience was originally a very small part only consisting of Hollywood Boulevard and Echo Lake. The intent was that the vast majority of the park would be experienced in a tram or through walking tours. When the park became wildly successful, then additional appendages were brought in. New York Street was originally a place for the tram to drive through, but it eventually became a pedestrian street. Other sections like Sunset Boulevard were constructed as additions. The result is that it has always struggled with having a well-thought-out Guest flow. Many times Guests either miss entire sections of the park, or they end up re-tracing their steps over the same areas repeatedly.

Disney California Adventure deals with the same issues as the Studios. Its layout is not conducive to an easy flow. Disney's Animal Kingdom allows you to bisect the park to get from one point to another, but it's by means of crossing over bridges into an island. At times you have to re-trace your steps in certain areas like Africa to get in and out of a particular area.

Go with the Flow – What is known is that the best-laid plans may still need changing. There is no substitute for what Guests tell you is the way to go. There is one story of gardeners at Disney who were upset with Guests cutting through a particular flowerbed in the park in order to get from one location to another. They were putting up barriers and signs to keep Guests from cutting through. Walt thought differently; he instructed the gardeners to install a sidewalk through the flowerbed. He trusted Guests to know the right way to go. It was simply a matter of getting out of the way and facilitating the right changes.

Create Emotional "weenies" – Walt Disney's concept of the "weenie at the end of the stick," is basically a form of wayfinding. If people see something that captures their attention, they will walk in that direction. Moreover, people will not only be drawn to them, they will rely on those iconic symbols to orient their movement. Castles and movie marquees, steamboats and mountains with coasters all have the same thing in common—they draw people to where you want them to go and help them find out where they are. People are curious and will go where you want them to go if you make it a place that piques their curiosity. These "weenies" also form anchors to better distribute the flow of your Guests so they are not all in one place at a time.

Move to the Right—Are you right-handed? Where you come from do you drive on the right hand side? If so, you may subconsciously tend to gravitate toward the right when you are searching for something you need. Disney knows that, and that is why they tend to place the products and services you need toward the right as you move in a given direction. Therefore, while the ticket gates at the Magic Kingdom are spread across the entrance, and while there are entrances to both the left and right, you find the lockers, as well as the entrance for strollers & wheel chairs towards the right.

For many years you could always find a Kodak store toward the right when you entered the park. That's because Kodak made certain that you would be stocked up with batteries, film and camera accessories as you start your day.

As you move further into the park, snacks for enjoying your day are available, such as candy, bakery goods and ice cream. There's even a Starbucks. The rest of the stores on the right side as you go down Main Street towards the castle are utilized by higher-end merchandise that will not be as crowded when you exit.

The movement toward the right is never more pronounced than when you leave the Magic Kingdom. What is always to the right as you exit? It's the gift shop—in this instance, the Emporium. They say the Emporium does more business in the last few hours of the day then the entire rest of the day combined. Why? Guests always pick up those last souvenirs on their way out.

Study any of the Disney parks, and you find most of these same principles applied.

Walk in the Shoes of the Guest – If you get lost trying to find something as an employee or manager, then I assure you that the Guest will likely become lost as well. You must walk in the shoes of the customer to understand how they are experiencing trying to find something.

Consider the park maps that are created to direct this experience. Originally they were laid out so that you saw the experience from the point-of-view of walking in the front gate. Even braille signs in the park are laid out in the same direction as the Guest is pointed.

But now Guests no longer primarily depend on the map. They also look at their smart phone. Therefore park maps have changed. With mobile GPS devices, the maps are placed in a North/South fashion, no matter where the entrance to the park is placed. That's because your mobile device will direct you in that same orientation.

The message, as always: Walk in the shoes of the Guest.

Make Your Tools for Wayfinding User-Friendly and Functional – When Epcot originally opened, Disney published a unique park map. In many ways it was a very cool map. Its design was unique – square, with a rotating dial that when turned would identify a specific location with a description of that location. It actually evolved from a similar style map used at Disneyland as a souvenir in previous years.

It was a great keepsake; the problem was one of functionality. The map was bulky and large, you couldn't fold it and put it in your pocket, it didn't even fit in most purses. People didn't know what to do with it.

After getting tired of carrying it around, they simply discarded it. You would find them lying around everywhere. The custodial teams quickly gave voice to their frustration in having so much extra waste to pick up. The message: Wayfinding must be friendly and functional. Today's park maps at Walt Disney World are oriented toward North, that's because they align to the electronic versions found in the MyDisneyExperience app that guests have on their mobile devices.

Bundle Key Services. Put the restroom, the drinking fountain, the ATM, mobile device charging stations and other similar services in the same location. That makes it not only easier for the Cast Member to remember where to direct the Guest to go, but it also serves many needs for a party that's together. One can go to the restroom, while the other plugs in their mobile device to get more battery life.

Use Words, Numbers, Symbols, and Colors – Those who really want a vacation from their vacation should grab a tube and float down Castaway Creek at Typhoon Lagoon. Not only is it a great way to kick back and watch the world go by, it's also a simple means for getting around the park easily. The trick is figuring where to get out. Disney made this easier by creating signage that includes four elements: a color, a shape, a word, and a number. Symbols and colors can be effective means of identifying a certain location or place.

Look for Those in Need—If nothing else, be proactive by having your employees looking for those Guests who look lost. Then try to help them get to where they need to be. Walk them to where they need to go if necessary. A great Take 5 is taking the time to help someone who can't find his or her way. Then learn from that and improve those places where customers are most likely to get lost. In a later chapter we speak of tip boards at Disney, which are located at key crossroads where Guests are most likely to have questions about which way to go.

Putting It All Together

Here's another example that shows how this works. During the early years at Walt Disney World, there was little cue that you had actually arrived at the Walt Disney World Resort other than signage that looked like it belonged in a national park. It was typical freeway signage, except the base color was National Park Brown instead of Highway Green. There was nothing emotive about arriving at Walt Disney World.

The company went about re-looking at all of its signage in the parks. They hired the group Sussman & Prejza, who had provided signage and wayfinding services for the Olympics in Los Angeles. They started by attaching colored ribbons around existing signposts. They then surveyed Guests coming through and asked them if they had seen any ribbons along the road. They noted those colors that stood out above others, and used them as the palette for designing the signage you see today throughout Walt Disney World. That same group provided wayfinding support to Disneyland Paris as it was built.

Later, they also re-visited the actual arrival experience. Some say that former Disney executive Michael Ovitz's key contribution to Walt Disney World during his short stay with the company was his remark on first arriving at Walt Disney World. Being unfamiliar with the property, he inquired as to where was it that you actually entered Walt Disney World. The end result was unique signage that heralded your arrival at Walt Disney World. This signage leads people where you want them to go. It is in many ways no different than the experience of seeing the Matterhorn from the freeway as you arrive at Disneyland. And while the original signage has long since been changed out, people still harken to the lettering and format that heralded the entrance itself into the parking lot. As a result, there can be a strong emotional connection with arriving at one's destination.

Wayfinding is a critical strategy for great customer service and for successful organizations. It's a blend between where you want your customers to go and what you want them to know, do, and feel, as well as where the customers themselves want to go and what they want to know, do and feel. So take these lessons from Disney in wayfinding, and show people the path to the magic.

What does wayfinding look like in your organization? It may not be a multi-million dollar focus, but it may be something you want to look at. Whether you're a small shop owner, an organization with locations found everywhere or even if you build web sites. All of these depend in some way on successful wayfinding techniques.

WAYFINDING & GUESTOLOGY YOUR WAY

LOOKING IN YOUR OWN MAGIC MIRROR, ASK YOURSELF:

- AM I WALKING IN THE SHOES OF MY CUSTOMER?

- AM I MAXIMIZING THE USE OF WORDS, NUMBERS, SYMBOLS, AND COLORS?

- AM I MAKING THE CHORE OF GETTING AROUND USER-FRIENDLY?

- DO I ENGAGE CUSTOMERS' EMOTIONS WHEN IT COMES TO FINDING THEIR WAY TO THE PRODUCTS AND SERVICES WE OFFER?

- AM I GOING WITH THE FLOW OF MY CUSTOMERS?

- AM I ANTICIPATING MY CUSTOMERS' NEEDS?

- WHAT PRODUCTS AND SERVICES ARE AVAILABLE AS GUESTS MOVE TOWARD THE RIGHT?

- ARE MY EMPLOYEES ON THE LOOK OUT FOR THOSE WHO ARE TRYING TO FIND THEIR WAY?

14

WAITING IN LINE AT DISNEY

THE HATE FOR THE WAIT

What is the biggest complaint Guests have of visiting a Disney theme park? Waiting in line. On opening day—known in Disney lore as *Black Sunday*—park Guests waited in line at Disneyland. They waited in line for food. They waited in line for merchandise. They waited in line for restrooms. They waited in line to go on rides. They waited in line to get into the park. They even waited so long just to get into the parking lot that first day that some of them were taking a bathroom break on the streets of Anaheim while waiting to get in!

Do you ever hate having to wait? We all wait at one time or another. But what makes waiting in one instance worse than another? That is the question to ponder, especially for those who have done their fair share of waiting in line at Disney.

Disneyland management knew on day one they had to do something about the queues. Just the line to the Jungle Cruise was going out the door to Adventureland and down Main Street U.S.A. One of the first things they learned is that having a switch back not only controlled the queue from ebbing into other areas of the park, but also created a perception that the line was not as long as one that stretched down one straight line. Since then, they have made waiting in line nearly an art form.

Let's identify the seven key challenges and solutions affecting the *perception* of wait time.

CHALLENGE #1: IS IT WORTH THE WAIT?

In the 1990's, a management decision was made that when one attraction was added to the park, another was deleted. After all, how big could a park get before you wanted to build another park? Thus, in time, several attractions familiar to the park Guests at the Magic Kingdom were out the door. Among them were the Skyway and 20,000 Leagues Under the Sea.

Many lament nostalgically that these attractions are no more, but those with clearer memories will recall that one of the primary reasons these attractions were chosen because wait times for those attractions were some of the worst in the park. Not that they were the longest, but they were often the slowest. Then, when you finally had the chance to ride, you were left with the question: "Was it worth the wait?" Honestly, the fact of the matter is, too many Guests did not feel that it was. In the case of 20K, many thought it would be *much* more than it was and came away disappointed. You have to make sure what you're offering is worth the wait.

The Solution: Make it Worth the Wait. There is a sliding scale for this problem called Value. Even Disney's best attraction is only worth so long a wait. Apple has many fans—individuals who willingly wait in line to be among the first to purchase a new iPhone or MacBook. The more value you create in the products and services you offer, the more worthwhile the wait.

When Disneyland re-commissioned its submarines in 2007, they went to great lengths to create greater value around the same ride experience. They added familiar characters from *Finding Nemo*, created a stronger story experience, added more visual and color appeal, and then loaded it with lots of special effects. You know you've achieved success when someone says, "it was worth the wait."

In short, there are many things you can do to improve the queuing experience itself. Of course, this chapter is not so much about the magic of Disney, but rather, the experience in *your* business or organization. What can *you* do for those who wait for the products and services you offer? What are you doing for your internal customers (employees) as well as for your external customers? Whatever you do, make it worth the wait.

CHALLENGE #2: UNOCCUPIED TIME FEELS LONGER THAN OCCUPIED TIME

As it was with Disneyland's first criticism, executives immediately went about creating a solution—and the best of these was to keep Guests busy while they waited.

Solution: Occupy their time. How does Disney occupy your time? In ways too innumerable to mention. But here are some of the most common:

- **Theme** – Indiana Jones Adventure, Splash Mountain, and Big Thunder Mountain all come to mind. Immersive settings make you feel like you're part of the attraction rather than just waiting for the attraction. No one does, or ever will, theme like Disney. It's the attention to detail—seeing something you hadn't seen the last time you stood in line--that makes the wait seem all that shorter.

- **Entertain** – A giant clock goes off every 15 minutes showcasing the time and creating a procession of dolls at "it's a small world." Banjo and guitar players entertain Guests waiting to board the Mark Twain Riverboat. Mountain climbers scale the mighty Matterhorn. All serve to entertain and distract Guests while they are waiting.

- **Educate** – Not as popular as entertaining, but it still works in terms of occupying attention while waiting in line. It might be a video about pineapple harvesting at the Enchanted Tiki Room. In America The Beautiful, the Hostess pointed at flags draped from the ceiling and asked who could name each banner. The original Great Moments with Mr. Lincoln involved a visual presentation of his life history as part of the pre-show.

These same ideas apply to any business setting. Providing free Internet access at the airport, or searching through the magazine rack at the supermarket while waiting to be checked out are all examples of this. What Disney has done is to take the queuing experience to a whole new level and maximize the wait experience. Maximizing the wait time is a big opportunity for any business.

CHALLENGE #3: PRE-PROCESS WAITS FEEL LONGER THAN IN-PROCESS WAITS

Millions of Guests enjoyed the Golden Horseshoe Revue with Slue Foot Slue and the gang, but does anyone remember the wait on the porch *outside* The Golden Horseshoe before you even got inside the restaurant? On a warm, sunny day, the wait seemed interminable, especially if you were in the stand-by line. You just stood in the sun, in one place, waiting for someone to let you in. In truth, the wait inside the restaurant for the show to begin was often longer, but it didn't feel like it because they kept you occupied inside by having you order your lunch. Involving someone in an activity, or processing him or her through some part of the experience makes the wait feel shorter.

Speaking of restaurants, that's the beauty of sit-down dining. Waiting at the bar for a table seems shorter than waiting outside for entry. The appetizer serves to occupy you while waiting for the main entrée to be prepared. Coffee or dessert serves to occupy you while you are waiting for your bill to be prepared.

Solution: Get them into the process immediately. When you feel like you're doing something, time goes much quicker.

This works well with new phone technologies. For instance, if I can provide key information via an electronic operator when calling about a hotel reservation, it saves me from having to spend that time on the back end when an actual operator comes on the line. It also occupies my attention and makes me feel like I'm not waiting as long. The downside is that if I provide information up front while I'm waiting for someone to answer, it's frustrating to be asked to repeat the same information on the back end by the operator.

Challenge #4: Anxiety Makes the Wait Seem Longer

How long before we get there? Are we there yet? The excitement and anxiety of traveling from Phoenix to Anaheim is still palpable to me. Thank goodness for my mom. She made sure there were lots of games, activities, and food to eat. She handled our excitement by keeping us busy whenever possible.

Solution: Settle their anxiety. Admittedly, there isn't much at Disneyland that creates anxiety, but when it happens, one has to address it. If you've ever waited in front of Sleeping Beauty Castle past the posted time for fireworks but didn't see anything happening, know that you are having a shared moment of anxiety with thousands of other park Guests. Far better to have someone over the speaker system announce a temporary setback. The same occurs in the Haunted Mansion, when our Ghost Host kindly explains that, "Prankish spirits have interrupted our journey; remain seated in your 'doom buggy.'" Any time someone is anxiously waiting, it's best to settle his or her anxiety.

I was a passenger on an airline not too long ago that was over an hour late boarding passengers. Then the plane spent nearly another hour waiting for room to pull out of the gate, and nearly another hour on the tarmac waiting its turn to take off. Passengers were frustrated and tired. I appreciated the flight attendants on board who decided to start the in-flight movie while still on the ground. It made everyone much less anxious as they passed the time.

Challenge #5: Uncertain or unexplained Wait Lengths Feel Longer than Known, Certain Wait Times

It's not hard to figure out how long the line is when one is standing in front of King Arthur's Carrousel or the Mad Tea Party. It's fairly obvious, because you can see everyone who is waiting, and you can see roughly how many teacups or horses. The challenge is when you really aren't certain how long the wait really might be. From the outside entrance of the attraction, you would not know how long the wait inside would be for the Indiana Jones Adventure. Conversely, a mere glance at the queue for Finding Nemo Submarine Voyage might not tell you how slowly that line flows. Having someone there to help explain the queue and the wait involved is important.

Solution: Provide certainty or explanation where possible. The anticipated wait time listed in front of any attraction is one of the best ways Disney handles this. Setting the expected time a little longer than the actual time also keeps the previously mentioned anxiety from building while waiting in the actual queue. In the case of attractions like Space Mountain where the entire queue cannot be viewed from any one location, having a greeter out in front helps to explain the length of time for boarding these longer-wait attractions. This also helps to allay uncertainty. Greeters can explain how long the wait may be and what options may exist. In the case of the submarines, they can educate park Guests about the longer boarding process for the submarines than for other attraction vehicles.

This principle also works very well when I'm on hold waiting for "the next available call center attendant." I appreciate it when the system actually tells me approximately how many minutes of wait time I can anticipate before my call will be answered.

CHALLENGE #6: UNFAIR WAITS FEEL LONGER THAN EQUITABLE WAITS

When customers perceive their wait is longer than someone else's wait, they become very impatient and irritable. That's why "butting" in line or letting someone go ahead angers so many.

Yet, some have special needs. It is unfair to ask someone who has difficulty walking to cover the entire length of a queue. And some queues are narrow, and difficult for someone in a wheel chair. Add to the challenge individuals who are Autistic, or simply don't have the ability to manage themselves emotionally in a queue. So over time,

Disney has made special allowance for them by providing a process that allowed them assistance or accommodation.

Yet, over the years, others have taken advantage of such processes. In time, people would rent a wheel chair with the idea that it would get them to the front of the line. Some have even gone so far as to hire someone who is disabled to accompany them in the park, so they can get special privileges.

Note how angry people can get when it's not fair. Take for instance a merging road where a driver will go around or ahead of others; such behavior quickly angers others. It's important to create ways to make it as fair as possible.

Solution: Make it as fair as possible. Disney has worked very hard to figure this out and to make it as fair as possible. First, by creating a queuing experience that doesn't facilitate or reward butting in line. Secondly, by creating a wait experience so enjoyable people would feel they were missing out if they didn't wait in line.

Still, Disney's had to really work harder in recent years by making it even fairer to all. So, wherever possible, Disney has started making the queue wide and accessible enough to allow everyone in a wheelchair party to progress through the queue together rather than move the party to the front.

These same ideas apply in the real world. For instance: the system of taking a number to be served by the butcher or baker (but not necessarily the candlestick maker) is a process that's been around a very long time. In another example, customers appreciate being told while on hold that my call will be answered in the order it was received. All these systems serve to help customers feel that they're being treated fairly.

CHALLENGE #7: SOLO WAITING FEELS LONGER THAN GROUP WAITING

Interacting with another individual is one of the best solutions for occupying time. It is also a great way to share any anxiety as it occurs.

Solution: Provide access to loved ones. This is another reason why the queue is better when it's wider. Why? Because you can talk to your friends and family while you're moving forward in line. It also makes it easier for parties with wheel chairs to be accommodated. Better yet, when you're in a holding area such as the train station or Mickey's PhilarMagic, you are then able to just cluster together and talk. All of which makes the wait seem shorter.

Hospital waiting rooms are an obvious example of why it's better to wait with someone you care for, rather than being by yourself. Remember when the dad-to-be used to wait it out while mom had the baby? Well, maybe you don't go back that far in time, but times, they sure have changed. Now sofa beds are placed in the room for dad when he gets tired. The end result is a completely different, shared experience when that baby is born. There are benefits in having access to loved ones while waiting — whether it's in the delivery room or the queue for Matterhorn Bobsleds.

CHALLENGE #8: WAITING AT ALL IS LONGER THAN NOT WAITING

Solution: Shorten or eliminate the wait. Outside of the "Happiest Place on Earth," people enjoy the benefit of not having to wait to pay a toll when heading down the highway. First it was simply a matter of slowing down going through a tollbooth rather than stopping. Now, technology lets them bypass the tollbooth altogether and head down the road at freeway speeds paying the toll electronically as they pass through. Anything that helps us not wait any longer than we have to is a boon to our busy lives.

At Disneyland we can all thank Dick Nunis for shortening the wait. In what was referred to as THRC, or the Theoretical Hourly Ride Capacity, he always pushed for rides and attractions that would maximize the capacity and move park Guests through more efficiently. Omnimover vehicles were a wonder back in the days of Adventures Through Inner Space! Creating larger excursion boats at Pirates of the

Caribbean moved park Guests quicker as well. Transporting park Guests to the Moon of Endor? Make sure you have plenty of simulators at Star Tours on hand to get everyone there in a reasonable period of time. Nunis also made sure that park personnel were moving Guests in and out of the ride vehicles as quickly and safely as possible so as to get as many people through as possible and reach that THRC.

Shortening the wait is good. Eliminating the wait is even better! And that brings us to the beauty of Disney's FastPass. FastPass is so revolutionary to the theme park experience that it has changed what we know as queueing in the parks. We'll cover that in the next chapter.

MANAGING HOW LONG A CUSTOMER WAITS

LOOKING IN YOUR OWN MAGIC MIRROR, ASK YOURSELF:

- HOW CAN I REDUCE OR SIMPLY ELIMINATE THE LINE?

- HOW CAN I OCCUPY THEIR TIME WHILE THEY ARE WAITING?

- HOW CAN I ALLOW OTHERS TO SHARE TOGETHER IN THE WAIT?

- HOW CAN I REDUCE THE ANXIETY OF WAITING?

- HOW CAN I CREATE SOME PRE-PROCESSING TO REDUCE THE WAIT?

- HOW CAN I PROVIDE CERTAINTY AROUND HAVING TO WAIT?

- HOW CAN I MAKE WAITING AS FAIR AS POSSIBLE?

- HOW CAN I MAKE IT WORTH THE WAIT?

15

HIGH TECH/HIGH EXPERIENCE

Technology is not a new thing to Disney. Walt consistently pushed the boundaries of technology since the early days of a black and white Mickey Mouse on through the advent of Audio Animatronics. Therefore, why not utilize technology to make the Guest experience better?

Technology has created new ways to make the Guest experience even better than before. In recent years Disney has invested over a billion dollars to make the Guest experience more high tech and better than ever. CEO Bob Iger made it one of three core strategic priorities when he took over Disney along with improving branded content and moving into international markets. Tom Staggs, serving as head of the Disney resort worldwide, noted: "The ultimate goal is to welcome more and more people, while making their experience more satisfying, more personal and more immersive." Let's look at ways in which Disney is providing its Guests more choices, more efficiencies, and more interactivity through technology.

HIGH TECH/HIGH EFFICIENCY

Efficiency and technology have been around a long time. It's what people think of when they think of high tech: How can we do something faster? How can we save time? Here's how Disney has approached it:

FastPass. A new technology solution appeared in the late 1990s. It came along when someone asked the question, "What if we gave them the option of not waiting in a queue?" The answer was a high-tech achievement known as Disney's FastPass. Simply go to one of several dispensers near the entrance to the attraction, insert your park ticket, and out comes a FastPass slip that designates a time that you can return and enter a separate queue that pulls you toward the front of the line. You are then free to go enjoy other attractions or experiences until the designated hour in which you are to return.

There's been much written about the pros and cons of Disney's FastPass. Many credit the service with saving them time to do more during a day, while others say that it has created longer lines at other attractions that don't include Disney's FastPass. Some have cited larger crowds mulling around now that they didn't have to wait in a queue. Some lament the loss of some of the time that they had beforehand with their family standing around in line. Those queues often provided them a captured moment just to converse with those they were with.

That being said, most would still take the FastPass. Disney's FastPass Service has given Guests the "gift of time." With time being as limited as it is in today's hurried world, people want to save as much time as possible. Disney's FastPass Service has been so successful that Disney has created a new generation of FastPass.

FastPass+. One of the problems around FastPass is that often a member of the family would run off to a particular ride or attraction to obtain FastPasses for their family. Then that member would return to their family only to have to retrace their steps when it was time to experience the attraction. What if you could set those FastPass times prior so you didn't have to run and obtain a FastPass before they were all handed out?

Enter FastPass+, where prior to coming to the park, Guests can now identify which of their favorite rides and attractions they would like to enjoy. From the comfort of their home they can obtain their FastPass times without having to physically run and obtain passes. Now additional rides, attractions, and even parade and fireworks locations have been added that allow Guests more choices about how they want to spend their time in the parks.

What if you're not a planning kind of person? There are still FastPasses that are available the day of. Moreover, if you get to Big Thunder Mountain and someone chickens out, you are able to change their FastPass to another choice.

MagicBands. To facilitate FastPass+ and to eliminate the need for a FastPass paper slip, Disney is providing Guests with what is referred to as a MagicBand. As Guests make plans in advance to visit Disney, they are sent a MagicBand. That band, fitting easily on their wrist, allows them to simply swipe as they enter those FastPass+ attractions.

But the MagicBand provides more. That same band allows them to easily enter the park itself. No more needing a ticket to enter. Wanting to purchase a Mickey ice cream bar? No need to pull out your wallet. Simply swipe your MagicBand. Wanting a Mickey plush as well? Swipe your MagicBand and charges will be forwarded to your account. Getting together for a picture in front of the castles? After the Cast Member shoots the picture so you can all be in the photo, swipe your MagicBand and you'll connect seamlessly to your PhotoPass account when you get to your room. Oh, and by the way, if you're staying on Disney property, the MagicBand will give you entry into your room— no need for a separate room key.

MagicBands offer new forms of convenience making it easier to do business with Disney. Efficiency and convenience are high tech solutions customers enjoy. But they're not the only ones. Customers also like to have options. And high tech choices are another form of Guest satisfaction. Let's look at that.

HIGH TECH/HIGH CHOICE

The Tip Board. It's the moment we stand at the end of Main Street, trying to figure out if we should head over to Tomorrowland or go to Frontierland. On a busy day, the risks are potentially high. We could go all the way over to Space Mountain only to find that the queue is over an hour. Then, frustrated, we turn to head over to Big Thunder Mountain or Splash Mountain, only to find that the queue might be longer than that. In the end, we find ourselves sitting out on all three attractions.

Then somebody had an idea: "Why not post a list of all the major attractions along with their wait times and let Guests make choices for themselves as to where they want to go?" Along came the glorious tip board. It was simple: Set up a marquee at the end of Main Street that would post wait times. Staff it with friendly Hosts who could answer the questions park Guests might have. Post additional information, show times, parades, and so on. *Voila!* The tip board is born. The technology wasn't so high tech—it was largely using radios—but it helped to provide Guests choices.

At the Magic Kingdom in Walt Disney World, it's called the "Main Street Gazette." At Disney's Hollywood Studios, the tip board is part of the Hollywood Junction of the Pacific Electric Railway, which also includes an area for reserving priority seating for meals. So successful was the use of these boards that smaller tip boards were added at different ends of the park, like in Harambe in Africa at Disney's Animal Kingdom.

MyDisneyExperience. With advances in technology, it only makes sense to ask, "why not give people those choices in the palm of their hand?" That's been the premise since the advent of the My Disney Experience mobile app. Millions have downloaded this software that allows them to look over Walt Disney World and find out what the wait times are. Tap a button labeled "Here and Now" and through GPS technology you're suddenly given a list of attractions, entertainment, restaurants and other park experiences near where you are standing. Now the tip board is in your hands.

HIGH TECH/HIGH TOUCH

Can I Talk to Mickey Mouse? It was simple—an opportunity to talk to Mickey Mouse, Donald Duck, Snow White and others by phone. It was in the post-show of America the Beautiful at Disneyland back in the late 1960's. It was really just a recording, but still, kids lined up to hear Mickey and the gang. Even today, you can ask a resort Host or Hostess, and they will have Goofy call you or a friend up on your birthday while staying at the resort. It's a simple thing, but it continues to delight.

Today Disney is more advanced than ever. Imagine being in a comedy show with monsters at the Monsters, Inc. Laugh Floor in Tomorrowland. It's really a standard improv routine—but you're interacting in real time with an animated monster on the screen—all the while being embarrassed by an array of antics.

Known as the Living Character Initiative at Disney, it is working to bring interaction to the experience of being at Disney. Imagine being able to talk to Mickey Mouse directly while getting your picture with him? Imagine if he knew your name as you approached? That would be pretty magical wouldn't it?

Your organization doesn't have Mickey Mouse or monsters. But imagine, if through technology, you could get better, more concise answers and solutions. Imagine if you could talk directly to the CEO when you had a complaint? Interactivity is about connectivity. Let technology be a means for bridging and building relationships more than ever.

Here's an example of how interpersonal this technology can be:

Turtle Talk with Crush. A few years ago, The Living Seas pavilion was renovated with a re-branding themed to the film, *Finding Nemo*. In doing so, they saw an opportunity to have Guests interact directly with the characters from the film in an encounter known as Turtle Talk with Crush.

The power of this experience came to me when I first visited Turtle Talk with my family. My daughter, nine at the time, raised her hand, gave her name, and asked Crush a question to which he responded. This experience alone of watching a cartoon character interact with my daughter was impressive. So much so that we got in line and came back to a later showing. As we sat through the second show, Crush recognized our daughter out of dozens of kids in that show and hundreds through that day, and called on her by name. While my daughter took it all in stride—"why wouldn't he remember me?"—we as parents were blown away and nearly in tears because Crush had managed to remember who our daughter was. It was simply an interactive experience that came alive.

Again, you may not have a Mickey Mouse or a Crush—but as AT&T oft suggested, you can still "reach out and touch someone." It's not just important to have technology, but to find new ways to interact with others. Disney sees that possibility with their MagicBands, where instead of messing around with tickets and wallets or running credit cards and counting change, its Cast Members can spend more time interacting with the Guest. Now transactions have a greater opportunity to become interactions.

Imagine the possibilities if every customer of yours walked away impressed not only with the technology you're provided, but also in the way you interacted with them. Consider further the possibilities if that technology could enhance that personal interaction.

HIGH TECH/HIGH EXPERIENCE

One of the most iconic attractions at the Magic Kingdom is Dumbo the Flying Elephant. There is seldom a child who sees Dumbo and doesn't want to take flight. Unfortunately, it has also been one of the most difficult waits in the park. Originally, the attraction had 12 elephants. It eventually was re-built to include 16 elephants. Still, the length of time waiting for only a few elephants at a time was painful given a confined space with little sense of movement. The circus-style tarp overhead offered relief from the rain, but still no relief from hot, sticky Florida summer days.

With the new Fantasyland, Dumbo was moved to the center ring of a new mini-land called Storybook Circus. Now, it fit more thematically than it did prior in a medieval-style setting. But with that opportunity came a chance to take the experience of waiting for Dumbo to a next level.

The most apparent change is that there is not one but two spinners, doubling the number of Dumbos from 16 to 32. FastPass was then added to the attraction allowing those wanting to go right on the ride the ability to nearly walk on to the attraction. But what about those who are waiting in stand-by--especially little children?

Instead of the previous switchback queue, an interactive tent was established. Guests waiting for Dumbo are given a restaurant-style pager while waiting. The tent is filled with an air-conditioned, circus-themed playground that invites kids to play. All the while, benches line the room inviting parents to sit back, relax, and let their kids play until it was their turn. When the pager sets off, you're invited to go and board Dumbo.

Now, no one waits around standing in the heat of the day for what was simply a carnival-style ride. In a new land with more Dumbos, FastPass, an interactive playground, plenty of seating and generous air conditioning, it has turned Dumbo the Flying Elephant into a complete Guest experience.

All this costs Disney money. But as a business, Disney recoups that investment because more people will be attracted to a company that pays attention not just on rides, but on the entire vacation experience. Guests will feel heard about their desire to not waste so much time in line. Wanting to take advantages of planning ahead, Guests will book their trips earlier, and will create a longer stay at the resort. With even little hassles removed like pulling out your wallet or purse, they'll be more inclined to make purchases on the fly. And when their hearts are won over by interacting with the magic of Disney, they will want to come back and do it all over again. It's a high tech/high experience.

Now if technology could only get your customers to do what you wanted them to do. It can, but customer compliance is much more than that, as we will see in our next chapter.

CREATING A HIGH TECH/HIGH EXPERIENCE

LOOKING IN YOUR OWN MAGIC MIRROR, ASK YOURSELF:

- HOW CAN TECHNOLOGY MAKE THE GUEST EXPERIENCE MORE EFFICIENT?

- WHAT HIGH TECH AND LOW TECH MEANS CAN OFFER CUSTOMERS THE GIFT OF TIME?

- HOW COULD I MAKE BETTER USE OF TECHNOLOGY TO IMPROVE CUSTOMER CHOICES?

- HOW DO I MAKE "HIGH TOUCH" A PART OF "HIGH TECH"?

- WHAT HIGH TECH/LOW TECH APPROACHES CAN I TAKE TO CREATE GREATER INTERACTIVITY AND CONNECTIVITY?

- HOW DO I UTILIZE TECHNOLOGY TO ENHANCE THE TOTAL GUEST EXPERIENCE?

16

GETTING GUESTS TO COMPLY

EXPECTATIONS MADE OF GUESTS

Think about your typical day at Disney. It's full of experiences where you may be the Guest, but Disney wants you to comply with certain expectations—many tied to safety. At any time, they want you as a Guest to:

- Not litter
- Clean up after yourself
- Utilize your Disney FastPass during the time allotted
- Stand behind the yellow line until the doors open
- Park your stroller in designated areas
- Restack your tray
- Not take unfair advantage of allowances made to Guests needing mobile assistance
- Not cut in line or in front of others
- Respect the experience of others
- Return your 3D glasses to the provided bins
- Not bring glass or alcohol into the park
- Trade only Disney pins with Cast Members
- Not go backstage
- Be on time for a reservation or priority seating

Mind you—we're not talking about breaking the law. This is not a chapter about shoplifting Mickey T's, utilizing a counterfeit park hopper ticket or even pulling on Tigger's tail. We're talking about general rules, policies, or procedures. Yes, the violation of those policies is protected by the legal wording of civility clauses on the back of the ticket and elsewhere. Anyone violating matters like this could conceivably be thrown out of the park. But it could get to a point that you create a police state monitoring these kinds of practices. And when you do that, you stop being the "happiest place on earth."

I have had countless service providers ask me about this. They're told, "The customer is always right." But then they see customers do things that aren't necessarily illegal, but are at least impolite, if not rude and disrespectful. How do you deal with addressing these customers and still maintaining the experience for everyone else?

Walt understood this. Walt understood that "cleanliness breeds cleanliness" and that if the right conditions were in place, people would feel obligated to seek after a trash receptacle to put their trash away. He appealed to the good in others, and felt that if you set the right tone, people would comply with what you were asking them to do. Here's an example from one Guest:

> "My family visits Disneyland in California often and last summer took our first trip to WDW. Being involved in scouts, my family always picks up trash wherever we see it - including in a Disney park. My boys have actually beaten Cast Members to the trash several times, with the Cast Members thanking them for helping to keep the park clean.

> "But it actually hasn't stopped there. Having a small retail store ourselves, when we go into shops we generally find ourselves straightening shelves, putting product that has been taken away from its sale area back where it belongs and generally helping out when we can. I can remember a very hot August evening at Disney-MGM Studios near closing when we came upon the Mr. Potato Head parts bar and found it woefully mixed up. We just set about putting everything back where it belonged and, even at closing time, the Cast Members came over to help and let us stay to help them finish the job! We actually had a great time hearing about the joys and perils of running a Disney toy shop!"

Walt was right! When you set a high standard, others will support you

114

in maintaining that level of quality.

The fact of the matter is that customers are are required to comply in the context of the products and services received. With that insight there are two ways of handling matters of compliance. One approach is enforcement—forcing them to do something—or else! The other method is one of getting people on board or winning them over to be compliant. Which is best?

There is a body of work out there that demonstrates that getting people on board to doing the right thing is far less expensive and is more effective than forcing them to do something. Yes! Winning compliance is better than enforcing compliance!

For even some Disney Cast Members, this is hard medicine to take. They've seen a darker side of the customer and they really don't buy into a winning compliance paradigm. From those individuals, it's not unusual to hear statements like:

- "You won't believe how rude Guests can be when you ask them to do something…"
- " Let me tell you how they trash that attraction while they're waiting in line…"
- "You have no idea what kids on Grad Nite will try to get away with…"

Yes…there are always those few who will do harm no matter how you treat them. And there should always be a consequence for such individuals. But there are solutions for getting the greater majority of good and honest customers on board to doing the things you ask of them. Here are several guidelines for how to get people to willingly comply with what you ask them to do. It's known as R.U.L.E.S. & Principles.

R.U.L.E.S.

R is for Relevant

Is it relevant that we adhere to this rule? Make certain that what you're asking customers to do really matters. Otherwise, don't hold them accountable for doing it. I mention this up front because some organizations create so many rules that they collapse from the weight of what they have to enforce. If the rule matters, then you are probably willing to do all of the other things I will suggest. If you find yourself not wanting to trouble yourself by doing those things, then perhaps you may not want to trouble the Guest in following that rule.

We should ask whether a customer is more correct as it applies to adhering to a given matter. Remember the story mentioned in the section on wayfinding. On one occasion, Walt found workmen at the park placing some sort of fencing around a garden/planter area. He inquired what was going on. The workmen said that Guests were cutting through and they were putting up a barrier to keep them from going through. He told them to trust where the Guests were moving, and to create a path that Guests could move through.

Now of course, there are planters and fences all over many of the parks. And the last thing we would want is to have Guests cutting through all over. But take your cues from the Guest. If there's something they consistently do, you may want to reconsider your enforcement of it.

U is for Uniform

Don't expect consistent compliance when you are constantly changing the rules. Perhaps one of the best examples of this is with the Transportation Security Administration at the airport. In some airports, they insist that you take off your shoes. At other airports, they care less about the shoes, and much more about removing the belt. If the principle were one of random security checking, one would understand. But if it's always one way at one airport and one way at another, it becomes confusing to those navigating through an already stressful experience. Add to this TSA attendants who are either yelling at the crowd that they should do this or that or correcting you because you didn't get it right. In one location if the shoes come off, they have to go in a bucket before going through the scanner. In other places, they're short of buckets, so they're frustrated if you don't put it directly on the belt. An occasional flier becomes stressed out, and even the frequent flier shakes their head in confusion. Uniformity supports customers in being compliant.

L is for Lead With Honey

You've probably heard the idiom that you can catch more flies with honey than vinegar. So it is with getting people to be compliant. Lead with honey, with kindness, not by using compulsive, controlling means.

MousePlanet editor, Lani Teshima, gave a great example of this as she described how Tokyo Disneyland Cast Members seek to lead others through patience and encouragement, rather than directive behavior. She writes:

"Reading your article made me think of the times I'd visited Tokyo Disneyland. You're standing up during a parade so you can get a better view. A Cast Member comes by and says, 'Very sorry for the intrusion but in order that everybody can have a good view of the parade we would like to ask that you kindly take a seat.' If you just stand there because Mickey's almost there and you wanted to take a picture of Mickey, the Cast Member will continue to stand there, and insist more insistently—"We apologize profusely, we are so very sorry, but in order that everybody can view the parade safely and in comfort, we please ask that you sit down please. Thank you very much." And on and on.

What a great example—and what a contrast to Disneyland who has an orderly system like no other for handling Guests during the fireworks and Fantasmic! But sometimes their manner is very direct, and quite loud—so loud that standing anywhere nearby all you hear is their shouting over the fireworks to move this way or that. Don't miss me on this. There is a time you must be direct. If I work at a zoo and I see children climbing into the pen of a dangerous animal, I'm going to be direct—even loud. After all, safety is first. But if we really think about it, we could in most instances of compliance use a lot more respect and sincerity.

Some say the customer is always right. Some say that Rule #1 is that the customer is always right and that Rule #2 is to read Rule #1. I disagree, and getting customers to comply is at the heart of why that isn't true. But while the customer is not always right, we should still treat the customer with as much respect as possible. You'll get more people to follow you if you lead with honey.

E is for Educate

It's a simple thing. Wash your hands when you're done using the restroom. So it seems silly that at the restroom sinks there are instructions on how to do so. And yet how many people really wash their hands after using the restroom--especially in the men's restroom?

Helping others understand the how and why behind compliance is important. Understanding the "why" is especially important. People by and large want to understand. To say, "Mickey says so" can be fairly lame. Much better is to use reason and to gently remind others of the actual benefit for doing something. And often the reason why is for one's own safety or for the greater good of all.

Returning to Lani's comments, she notes the following:

> "Japan as a culture is very compliance-driven because you have such a dense population living close together in such a small geographical space (half the population of the United States stuck in a space the size of California, with most of it consisting of uninhabitable mountains).

> "When you do something they don't want you to do in Japan, the Cast Members kind of remind me of the insistent little cleaner robots in Pixar's *WALL-E*. They are extraordinarily polite. In fact, the more you resist, the more polite they get. But

they are also quite firm in explaining why they need you to comply. And you know what? They never tell you to change your behavior because they want you to. They tell you it's for the comfort and safety of everyone around you. So there you have it: Self control through social conformity!"

S is for Support

There are a number of things one can do to support a culture of compliance. Going back to the example just given, you can reward those who keep those rules by providing them a great Guest experience.

Epcot made changes to its security entrance to better manage the flow of Guests stepping off the tram and entering the park via a bag check. Nothing inherently wrong with that—it actually makes sense. But if that's your design, then you better support the experience with enough courtesy trams to pick up Guests and drop them off. To charge a fairly high amount of money to park your car, to direct cars as to where you want them to park, and then to not provide a courtesy tram in a reasonable amount of time (and I would say that if you can walk all the way from the back of the parking lot to the front without being afforded a courtesy tram to be unreasonable), then you deserve hot, tired individuals walking straight through unmarked entrances instead of veering in a whole different direction to enter via the courtesy tram drop off. This point cannot be emphasized enough—you must support the rule if you want people to adhere to it!

These are the R.U.L.E.S. Use them and you will find people are far more compliant. Better yet, more than acting from R.U.L.E.S., act from…

PRINCIPLES

It is far better to be principle-centered than rule-governed. Be careful you are not acting from a culture of wanting to control everything that goes on. Let me offer an example of this that harkens to my days operating a major water park. The owner asked that I create new signage for all of the slides and pools. I thought about how much signage should be created, and what should be written on the signs. I went over to Typhoon Lagoon to see how they did it. I was surprised that the signage had little verbiage. There were perhaps only two to three things that were noted on any sign. Contrast this to what my owner wanted to do. His list went anywhere from 7-12 items per sign. Now take the average kid going through the park. Who is going to read a sign that long, much less one sign after another?

But you say, "Wait—what if we don't list the rule and they do something wrong—how can you hold them accountable?" Let's just say that when it comes to a water slide and a pool, you can brainstorm more ways than you can count as to how to be unsafe. You don't have signs enough to count all the ways. At some point, you have to just say, "be safe," and then do the things we've mentioned prior to reinforce acting safely. If there are a couple of things that occur frequently, point those problems out. But stay principle-centered.

Those are some key lessons about getting customers to comply. It's not an easy matter. In fact, it's one of the most challenging aspects of customer service-trying to get people to do something, while still creating an experience so amazing and wonderful that they want to come back to what you have to offer again and again.

CREATING CUSTOMER COMPLIANCE

LOOKING IN YOUR OWN MAGIC MIRROR, ASK YOURSELF:

- WHERE ARE CUSTOMERS EXPECTED TO COMPLY WITHIN YOUR OPERATION? WHAT ARE THE ACTIVITIES CUSTOMERS DON'T LIKE TO DO?

- ARE THE POLICIES PUT IN PLACE REALLY NEEDED? ARE THEY KEEPING CUSTOMERS FROM WANTING TO DO BUSINESS WITH ME?

- HOW CAN I MAKE THESE CUSTOMER EXPECTATIONS MORE UNIFORM?

- HOW CAN I LEAD BY INFLUENCING OTHERS TO DO WHAT THEY NEED TO DO RATHER THAN IMPLEMENTING CONTROLS?

- WHAT CAN BE DONE TO BETTER EDUCATE AND COMMUNICATE THOSE POLIICIES AND CUSTOMER REQUIREMENTS?

- HOW CAN I BETTER SUPPORT CUSTOMERS IN THEIR DOING WHAT IS BEING ASKED OF THEM?

- HOW CAN I BE MORE PRINCIPLE-CENTERED IN OUR APPROACH TO GETTING OTHERS ON BOARD TO DOING THE RIGHT THING?

- WHERE DO THESE ISSUES SHOW UP INTERNALLY AS WELL AS EXTERNALLY?

17

SERVICE NETTING

JUST DIAL 911

Consider this analogy. Envision yourself at Cirque du Soleil's *La Nouba* in Downtown Disney. One of the best parts of the show is the spectacular team of trapeze artists. They are excellent—even phenomenal—but even the best performers risk the possibility of falling at some point.

Imagine that the management at *La Nouba* decides (because of the cost and hassle) not to provide a net—after all, it's the trapeze artist's fault if they fall! Management is willing to install a sign near the phone backstage to call 911 in the event of an emergency. In fact, they even say that should anyone need to call, let management know, and they will call 911 themselves (that way, we don't have people calling unnecessarily).

Sound ridiculous? Certainly, but the analogy emphasizes how organizations typically fix customer service scenarios. They provide for service recovery in the event something goes wrong. They stress that management should handle service recovery so that no one takes advantage of the system.

The fact is that customers will experience challenges—including mistakes of their own making. Proactively anticipating issues and challenges is a term I call "Service Netting." Responding after the fact is often referred to as "Service Recovery." There should be both a net and a phone on hand, but most only think about the response afterwards, rather than creating a net so that the crisis, or the customer's dissatisfaction, doesn't happen in the first place.

Disney does many things that act as service nets to keep customers from having problems later on. Some—such as the tip boards near the front and center of each park--allow Guests to make choices as to how they want to spend their time so they aren't frustrated walking all over the park only to discover long queues at their desired destination.

Here are some other excellent ways Disney approaches service netting. Many of these are processes that make it easier for Guests to do business with them. Let's take a look:

REMOVE SERVICE BARRIERS

Picture your arrival midday at China in Epcot's World Showcase. As you shop through the streets and stores, you discover a beautiful ivory statue. It's perfect for your home. You would like to purchase it, but were planning on spending the rest of the day in the park. What do you do? Do you purchase it and carry it around all day? Do you take it back to your car? Do you wait and come back at the end of the day? What if you aren't passing by the store later? What if the store has closed by the time you return? Making such a purchase like this may feel punitive rather than rewarding.

The good news is that Disney removes the service barriers to buying your dream statue. They provide a service that allows you make your purchase and then pick up the item as you exit the park later in the day. Resort Guests can even pick up their purchases at their hotel the following day. For a nominal fee, Guests can even make arrangements to have it shipped directly home. It's all part of removing service barriers for their customers.

Ask yourself, what barriers keep our customers from taking advantage of the products and services we offer? What no-cost, low-cost, or cost-competitive options can we offer that support the services we provide?

PREVENT SERVICE RUN-AROUNDS

Have you ever experienced the following?

- Waiting for people to get back to you with the answer you need.
- Having to dial through an endless phone tree to get your response.
- Being shuffled from one department to another.
- Being told "We don't handle that" or "We're just the vendor."

We all hate service runarounds. Anticipating and providing solutions so the customer doesn't have to experience any runarounds is an important part of providing exceptional customer service.

Here's what that looks like at Disney. Suppose your child loves Pocahontas and wants to visit with her. Where can you go to see Pocahontas? At Walt Disney World, she could be many places: she could be in a parade, she could be in Disney's Animal Kingdom, she could be in the Magic Kingdom, and she could be at a character meal in Disney's Wilderness Lodge. Where do you go and when?

Ask any Cast Member! They have access to a special phone number; the last four digits spell CHIP, as in the rambunctious Disney characters, Chip and Dale. By calling that number, Cast Members can find out where any Disney character may be on any occasion. This not only removes the service runaround, it makes that Cast Member a hero to that family—all because they were armed with the solution they needed to help support the Guest experience.

Consider for yourself, what service process in our organization requires streamlining so that customers aren't helpless in getting the support they need? How do we communicate those one-stop service solutions so that both the customer and the employee know where to go? How have we set the expectation that we must take responsibility to follow through on calls, rather than passing it off to others?

INSTALL REDUNDANT SERVICE SYSTEMS

You are in Tomorrowland in the Magic Kingdom. You want to take your child on their very first ride on Space Mountain. You get to the attraction and there's an hour wait with no FastPass available. No matter, you came to ride Space Mountain, and ride it you will...so you get in line and wait. When you get to the very front of the queue and are preparing to board, you are told your child is too short to ride. You become frustrated and upset that you've waited in line for so long and now you are being turned away.

Of course, Disney works hard to keep this from happening. First of all, they do many things to communicate the height requirements of the attractions. They're stated at the entrance to the attraction, stated at the tip board, stated in the park guides and on MyMagic+, and if that isn't enough, they staff a greeter to anticipate such situations. With these redundant service systems in place, the cumulative effect largely removes the chance a child will wait in line only to be turned away.

What if a child wanting to ride the attraction still gets to the ride and finds out that the attraction has a height requirement and can't board? As a recovery measure, greeters have access to a special card, themed to Space Mountain and signed by Mickey Mouse himself that guarantees the child and his or her party may go to the front of the line and board the attraction when the child has reached the appropriate height.

Ask yourself, what redundant systems do we have in place to support those customers who are not successfully getting through the system? What processes do we have in place to make certain that a customer doesn't get too far along before realizing that particular products or services are not available to them?

CONSIDER THE NET EFFECT

We all have need of building service nets in our own organization--even Disney isn't perfect. We all can do more. Let's suppose we're over at the Disney Reservation Center. Much management time is spent trying to figure out how to reduce the amount of time customers wait on hold before their calls are answered. Leaders monitor calls to keep them as brief as possible to reduce the number showing the average length of call. The organization also wants to increase the number of staff to further reduce the wait Guests might have.

There is nothing inherently wrong with doing this. But consider the following:

- What if a call center Cast Member took a little more time for those who really needed the help? Wouldn't it keep the customer from perhaps calling again later?

- What if we focused more of our attention on identifying solutions that give customers the information they need so that they don't have to call the customer service hotline in the first place?

That kind of focus is service net-oriented rather than the service recovery scenario founded on how to handle customers when they call in with their problems.

Take a look at your own organizations. You'll find that nets can be some of the most powerful magic you can create in your own business.

BUILDING YOUR OWN SERVICE NETS

LOOKING IN YOUR OWN MAGIC MIRROR, ASK YOURSELF:

- WHAT SAFETY NETS COULD I PROVIDE TO MY CUSTOMERS? (EVEN WHEN IT'S THEIR FAULT AND THEY MADE THE MISTAKE?)

- WHAT AM I CURRENTLY DOING TO PROVIDE SERVICE RECOVERY? WHAT COULD I DO TO ANTICIPATE THIS PROBLEM BEFORE IT OCCURS?

- WHAT ARE MY CUSTOMERS/COMPLIERS MOST OFTEN COMPLAINING ABOUT? HOW CAN I RESPOND PROACTIVELY?

- WITHIN THE ORGANIZATION , WHO DO I NEED TO COLLABORATE WITH TO MAKE THIS HAPPEN? WITH WHOM DO I NEED TO COMMUNICATE? WHERE DOES THIS SHOW UP INTERNALLY AS WELL AS EXTERNALLY?

- WHAT DO I NEED TO DO DIFFERENTLY TO HOLD UP MY PART OF THE NET? WHAT CONVERSATIONS NEED TO TAKE PLACE WITH THOSE NOT HOLDING UP THEIR PART OF THE NET?

18

PROVIDING SERVICE RECOVERY

"I FORGOT WHERE I PARKED!"

A previous chapter spoke of Service Netting—creating solutions to customer situations before they became problems (at which point they become Service Recovery). I gave the analogy of having a net in place for a high wire act, rather than just a direct line to 911.

Let's see these concepts in action by spending some time at Epcot. Epcot is an amazing place. It's exciting to look up and see Spaceship Earth as you arrive by car. You enter certain sections of the lot like Journey, Discover, or Amaze, park your car, board a tram and then pass through the turnstiles.

You head off into the park to enjoy the rides and attractions throughout Future World and the World Showcase. You enjoy a number of attractions, do some shopping, take in a fine meal and cap off the day by seeing IllumiNations.

As you head out to your car at the end of the day you think that Epcot should really be an acronym for "Every Person Comes Out Tired."

It's then that you realize you've forgotten where you parked.

There are over 11,000 parking spaces at Epcot... A vast space so large you could plop a small island nation into it. What do you do? What are your options?

You could:

- Wait until the end of the night and your car is the only one left.
- Split up your family to search all the sections of the parking lot.
- Press the beeper on your key chain until you hear your car start honking.

Ask yourself:

- How many of you would think to find a Cast Member and ask them where your car is parked?
- Whose fault is it that you lost your car? Should Disney be responsible for the fact that you lost your car?
- Should you expect Disney to do anything about it?

In the spirit of the concept of Service Netting mentioned earlier, it should be mentioned that Disney labels each section and row of the parking lot and, when you board your tram, they mention where you parked your car—not once, not twice, but three times.

Is Disney therefore still responsible? If so, should Disney do something about it? If not, should Disney still do something about it? Before you decide, consider the following: How many times have you heard someone around your office or business say: "It's their fault! They're the ones to blame. They made the mistake. They have no one to blame but themselves."

In our own work environments, there are many times where the situation is not our fault. Great service lies in being the hero, even though it really isn't your fault, but rather the fault of the customer or another employee.

So going back to our situation at Epcot, what do you do?

Well, imagine approaching a Cast Member and saying, "You won't believe this...in fact, you probably never had this happen before... but I forgot where I parked my car."

The Cast Member asks: "What time did you arrive this morning?

"A little after 10:00 a.m."

"Just after 10:00, we were parking rows 22-24 of the Imagine parking lot. Let's help you over there so you can find your car."

Now how did they know that?

Unbeknownst to your family, while you were busy boarding the tram and getting excited about entering Epcot, the tram driver was taking a small one-page map of the parking lot and noting the time they parked rows 22-24. Later in the day, the manager took the marked map, made copies for all the Cast Members, and handed them out to everyone working in the parking lot—including the Cast Member you just approached.

Who do you think came up with this idea? The Cast Members who were working in the parking lots! This simple safety net costs little to implement but creates great service results.

Disney didn't have to do that. After all, it was the customer's fault they forgot where they parked the car. Imagine putting all that effort into creating an experience like Epcot, only to have a customer's day ruined because they forgot where they parked their car.

On the other side of the Service Net coin we find Service Recovery. When the Service Net no longer holds, it's time to take action to provide recovery.

ENTER SERVICE RECOVERY

No matter how proactive we are, or how strong our Service Nets, sometimes we make mistakes. A loophole is created in a certain policy, numbers get crunched incorrectly, the fire alarm goes off, we forget to pass on an important message, or we miss a step while tidying up a showroom. Mistakes are made because we're imperfect people. We need to be prepared to react to these situations appropriately. If we don't react appropriately, it can have significant impact on our customers, which in turn will have a significant impact on our bottom line.

Dissatisfied customers typically tell more people about their experience than satisfied customers. Did you know that most of those same customers tend not to complain to the service provider? It's often your advocates that will complain, because they care about your business and want it to succeed. In reality, less than one percent of customers are trying to "scam" your business.

The following is a grid originated by my colleagues Dennis Snow and Guy Smith to help employees make decisions in the moment as to how they should serve others as they handle a myriad of situations everyday.

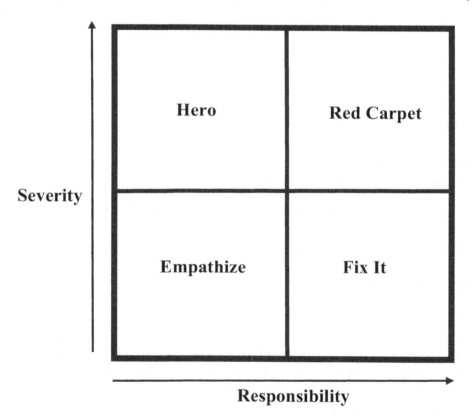

This Service Recovery model is a matrix that represents a combination of two different situation criteria. Those two criteria are severity and responsibility.

Severity – How bad is the situation? How much has it affected our ability to deliver great products and services to our customers?

Responsibility – How responsible are we for what has occurred? This is the moment we have to look at our accountability. We do this not to judge or point blame, but to make certain that we do not jeopardize trust because we haven't been forthright about our responsibility. It's about fixing systems, not fixing blame.

Given these two criteria, let's walk through the four matrix sections to see how we apply the service standards discussed earlier:

EMPATHIZE

In this situation, you're making a small effort to help another. You know what it's like when you can't make it happen yourself. Here are some examples:

- Plans for being out in the park are halted by a major rainstorm. Apologizing about the weather, you offer other ideas about what can be done indoors.
- A Guest visits a hospital, only to become confused as to where to go. You point the way, or better yet, lead them there.
- A customer calls the wrong department. Rather than telling them they're wrong, you look up the correct number, provide that number to them and then try to connect them to the right party.

FIX IT

This situation is one in which the matter is hardly serious. However, it is one that necessitates that the matter be fixed, since the responsibility for it is significant. Consider the following situations:

- A seat in coach is double-booked on a plane. The airline offers another vacant seat to you. They may even offer a seat in first class if available.
- You receive a double billing on your electrical bill. You bring it to the attention of the utility and they credit your account immediately.
- Your nametag is misspelled. They send you a corrected one.

RED CARPET

In this section, both the responsibility and the severity or seriousness of the matter is extreme. These dire circumstances should be rare, but the service accountability is very high and necessitates extra efforts of those responsible to make up for it. Consider the following situations:

- A nearby construction crew splatters cement on cars in the adjacent parking lot. The construction company offers to sand and repaint the damaged vehicles. Car rentals are offered while the cars are in the shop.
- The airline loses your bags while on vacation. They provide you funds to replace the items you lost and need in order to continue to enjoy your vacation.
- A cruise ship loses all engine power while on the seas leaving you out on the ocean an extra day. It provides extra care support during the time it takes to get you and others back to shore. It refunds your experience, gets you a new airline booking, and comps you a free cruise in the future.

HERO

This is the quadrant where nearly all businesses fail to capitalize on an incredibly valuable opportunity. Here the situation is such that it isn't the fault of the company. But providing service recovery—particularly when the need is serious and the customer is at their most vulnerable—can make heroes of those who provide that support and relief. These are the moments when nearly all legendary businesses break from the ordinary and become world-class. Here are some examples:

- A kid drops an ice cream cone before leaving the cone shop. To the child the world has ended. The shop owner gives the child a new cone for free.
- Your insurance provider hears that your home burned down this morning. She comes out to your home site bringing not only a check but also dinner and some miscellaneous supplies to help the family get through the situation.
- An airline provides a direct link to an on-call doctor available to the aircrew in the event that one of their passengers falls seriously ill on the plane and needs immediate medical attention.

Our parking lot story fits in here. To an exhausted family ready to drop dead back at their hotel room, it seems overwhelming to realize that they have no clue where the car is parked. While there are nets in place to help them not to forget where they parked the car, and while it's not Disney's fault that they lost that car, Disney still comes to save the day. All of this tiers up to creating greater Guest loyalty. And Guest loyalty drives the bottom line.

OFFERING CUSTOMERS SERVICE RECOVERY

LOOKING IN YOUR OWN MAGIC MIRROR, ASK YOURSELF:

- HOW IMMEDIATE CAN I PROVIDE SERVICE RECOVERY?

- HAVE I EMPOWERED MY FRONT LINE STAFF TO PROVIDE THAT SERVICE RECOVERY?

- HOW CAN I CREATE GREATER OPPORTUNITIES TO BE THE HERO?

- AM I DEVELOPING SERVICE NETS FROM THESE SERVICE RECOVERY EXPERIENCES?

19

PROVIDING SERVICE THAT L.A.S.T.s

STATIN' THE BACON AT LIBERTY TREE TAVERN

In the previous chapter I spoke about providing great Service Recovery. I talked about four ways to respond to an incident based on the severity and whose responsibility it was for what happened. I shared examples of Service Recovery in action. Now let's extend the conversation further to discuss how best to redress a customer service challenge.

On one occasion I hosted a group of executives on a benchmarking program in Orlando. We dined for lunch at the Liberty Tree Tavern in the Magic Kingdom at Walt Disney World. The conversation turned to those who are operating partners with Disney, and the expectation Disney has of those third party relationships. One of our participants related an experience that occurred to her several years ago. She was dining in Downtown Disney at one of the third party restaurants there. Her associate asked for a Piña Colada, so she requested one as well, only she emphasized to the server that it have no alcohol since she had an extreme allergy.

She was served a virgin Piña Colada, but the drink was blended in a mixer that had not been rinsed out properly. She immediately went into an allergic reaction and had to be taken to the closest hospital for proper care.

The general manager of the restaurant took immediate action and responsibility, calling on her personally, and offering his concern. He took ownership of any bills associated with the event, and invited her and her colleague back to the restaurant for a free meal at any time in the future. She thanked the manager, but stated she was from out of state and did not plan on returning any time in the near future.

Fast-forward a year later and my colleague was back at Walt Disney World with some associates attending a conference. They found themselves in Downtown Disney and decided that they would return to the restaurant where she had dined previously. She didn't think they would remember the incident, much less provide the offer of a free meal, but decided to inquire anyways. Checking at the podium, she asked for the manager on duty and gave her name. The podium attendant immediately responded to the name without any other prompting, stating that her incident was well known at the restaurant and that the experience had resulted in serious staff training over the last year. He went to get the duty manager, who attended to her every need, rolling out whatever red carpet he could and thanking her for returning to the restaurant. Moreover, the general manager of the restaurant, who was at home that evening, found out and he himself came over to the restaurant to attend to her personally.

She was wowed by the experience because of how they took responsibility and treated her accordingly. Equally impressive, is that in the wake of that experience, they built a strong safety net to prevent such events from happening again.

Now if that were not enough, in an irony of ironies, just minutes after the one participant related this story at our table at the Liberty Tree Tavern, another participant threw her sandwich on the plate, and exclaimed that the sandwich had bacon. This participant was allergic to bacon, which was hidden beneath layers in a Salmon Club Sandwich.

I asked what needed to be done. She said she needed some Benadryl, so I quickly escorted her to First Aid to get some medication. She hadn't consumed much of the sandwich, and she wasn't sure what the effect was. The Cast Member at First Aid was attentive, and emphasized that they would get her additional attention if she needed to go to the hospital. Upon returning to the restaurant, she asked to stop and rest for a moment in the front of the restaurant. While she did, I went back in to attend to the other participants. There I found the duty manager and chef speaking to the group. I listened only long enough to hear the duty manager respond defensively to the situation at hand. Her response was: "Everyone knows that a club sandwich has bacon in it." Our participants were stating: "Why doesn't it say that it has bacon on the menu? It goes into detail about the bun being toasted multi-grain and that the mayonnaise was 'lemon-basil.' But it says nothing about bacon?"

I pulled the manager to the side, explaining to her that I was the leader of the group. While I didn't tell her that I was a former Cast Member, I did urge her to focus on the well-being of the victim and to not posture herself defensively. I directed the manager to the participant now seated in the lobby. The participant felt that perhaps it would be best if she went to the hospital. The ambulance from Reedy Creek Emergency Services was called and she was back-doored out of the park behind Frontierland and taken to the local urgent care center. There my business partner met her and attended to her needs.

I'm happy to say that the participant not only recovered from the experience, but returned later that evening to join up with our group. I'm glad she took the necessary precautions. On the other hand, the duty manager's response was by no means "Red Carpet." She offered to remove the participant's meal cost from the bill, as well as mine, which I found so token I didn't even want to address the matter. She did call later to inquire about the participant, but again, it seemed to be merely a matter of checking off something from her list of steps managers were required to take under such circumstances. I never heard her express sympathy for the participant--much less rise to the level to which a Disney Cast Member ought to rise.

I've pondered the incident since then, and wondered why the manager's response was tepid at best. First, I think it had to do with the grid we spoke of in our first chapter on Service Recovery.

I feel the incident was taken seriously, so clearly severity was not the issue. But there was still that sense of responsibility. It doesn't really matter whose fault it was that the individual consumed the bacon in the sandwich unknowingly; one should respond either by pulling out the Red Carpet or by stepping forward to be a Hero. Their defensive response, suggesting that she should have *known* that a "club" sandwich would obviously have bacon in it, gave the unwelcome message: "It's her own fault; she should have figured that out in the first place."

It's not too different than: "It's their fault they lost their car. They should have remembered where they parked it—especially after we told them three times on the tram not to forget where they parked!"

Which is why our experience with the parking lot is so amazing. They approach the same kind of experience with a solution for being the Hero of the day—even when it's not Disney's fault.

It wouldn't have really mattered if the manager had responded to the incident by being a hero or by pulling out the red carpet. Instead, the approach was more token... more a response to protecting one's self legally, rather than identifying opportunities to create loyal customers.

MAKE IT L.A.S.T.

How should the manager have treated the matter? There's an acronym for it—L.A.S.T. And what does L.A.S.T. stand for?

Listen – Let the customer share what happened. Let them vent if need be. Let them get it out. Don't rush to answer. Maintain good eye contact and open body language. Ask open-ended questions. Capture the critical details. Consider how the Guest's emotions are influencing their words. Make certain that the customer feels completely heard before you start offering solutions.

Apologize – Express sincere disappointment for the situation not meeting their expectations (no excuses, no blame) and affirm that you are committed to doing whatever is in your power to make it right. This is not so much about stating you are wrong, but rather expressing empathically your concern about the situation.

Solve – Find the right solution and provide it immediately. This is where the grid makes the most sense. If it's a case of offering Empathy, do so. If the matter needs to be fixed—fix it! Most important, roll out the Red Carpet if you're at all to blame, or be a Hero in some way even when it's not expected.

Thank – Often, the best gifts we receive from customers are the complaints they register. Feedback is the breakfast of service champions. While it isn't human nature to appreciate negative comments, those complaints can act as a road map to tell us if we're on track to providing the quality of service we want to offer. Being genuine and authentic is critical in thanking them. Doing something about it to make sure it never happens again is even paramount.

There was little (if any) L.A.S.T. coming from the manager on duty at the restaurant. Nor was her response unique: I encountered similar responses from other people involved. While the folks at Reedy Creek Emergency Services were right on cue, the chef acted just as defensively. A couple of other area managers called to assist at the scene were also emotionally detached. One of them was someone I had worked with 10 years earlier when I worked in that small office above the Italy pavilion. He remembered me, but not once did he approach me or my Guest with the least bit of genuine concern. I felt like I was just another number on the way out the back door. Once the ambulance moved on, I approached the manager I knew and we spoke for a moment about where our careers had taken us, but never once did he ask questions or express concern about the individual in need.

I thought about this for some time afterwards. My guess as to the reason these kinds of behaviors occur in service industries is that there is often a strong emphasis by a corporate legal team that management be very careful about what they say or what they offer. Or, I find in instances like these, that middle management receives so little empathy for their own situation that they find it difficult to offer it to others.

Don't mistake me—there are so many great stories I've heard across Disney property about Cast Members who went the extra mile—and some are listed in this book. This is one of the key ingredients for creating great service, and with millions of people returning to Disney every year they must be doing something right.

MAKING SERVICE NETS

For that matter, my tri-cornered hat is also off to most of the wonderful Hosts and Hostesses that make up the Liberty Tree Tavern. I've eaten there enough times to know that they really *can* make the magic themselves. There's even something positive to be said about the management. Two months later, we took another group for lunch at the Tavern and I was anxious. The last thing I wanted was to check another one of our participants into the hospital, but other restaurants in the park were unavailable, or were simply not the right fit for our needs.

So I rejoiced when I got there and took a look at the new menu. Yes, there was a revised menu stating bacon was on the sandwich—and that's no ordinary bacon, that's Applewood Smoked Bacon! More humorous was that as one of the participants at our table ordered that very same sandwich, the Hostess went into an automated spiel about the sandwich having bacon, only to stop mid-sentence and say: "Oh, I don't have to say that any more...they changed the menu."

Was the inclusion of bacon on the menu enough of a net? I'm not sure. Last I dined there, the item had since been entirely removed. Perhaps there had still been other incidents. What matters is taking those service recovery incidents and making nets out of them.

As for service recovery, whose responsibility is it? Does it matter? It doesn't if having a great Guest experience is your goal. So consider that when it's necessary in your own organization to either roll out the Red Carpet or become a Hero yourself. It's the only way to make the magic in your own business.

MAKING YOUR SERVICE L.A.S.T.

LOOKING IN YOUR OWN MAGIC MIRROR, ASK YOURSELF:

- HOW AM I LISTENING TO MY CUSTOMERS WHEN THEY COMPLAIN?

- DO I ALLOW FOR APOLOGIES ON MY BEHALF?

- CAN I NOT ONLY SOLVE A CUSTOMER COMPLAINT, BUT ALSO CREATE NETS TO PREVENT THOSE COMPLAINTS FROM HAPPENING IN THE FUTURE?

- WHEN'S THE LAST TIME I THANKED MY CUSTOMERS FOR THEIR FEEDBACK?

- NO MATTER THE RESPONSIBILITY, DO I MAKE CERTAIN THAT I EITHER PROVIDE RED CARPET OR HERO TREATMENT?

20

THREE LESSONS IN SERVICE RECOVERY

LESSON 1: EMPOWER THE FRONT LINE TO RESPOND IMMEDIATELY

In my last few chapters I've spoken about Service Recovery. Let's drive home this discussion on Service Recovery with three important lessons. Here are some examples not only from Disney, but also from other major service organizations, to illustrate the lessons.

Suppose your child purchases an ice cream but then drops it as she's exiting Carabelle's Hand-Scooped Ice Cream store on Buena Vista Street. A Cast Member walking by should be able to escort your child back to the store and help you to get another cone—without needing to ask permission of the Cast Members in that facility, much less the duty manager. Great organizations empower their front line employees to deliver Service Recovery rather than handing such matters over to management. There are several reasons why this works best.

1. The more immediate the recovery, the more the customer feels acknowledged. The longer they wait, or the more hoops they have to go through to get that recovery, the more they will feel unappreciated as customers.

2. Immediate service recovery not only helps companies to retain their customers, it keeps the employees around as well. This is because they're empowered through training to make decisions that will satisfy their customers. Feeling like they have been Heroes to customers can make them feel extremely satisfied.

On the average, front line employees who are trained do a better job offering Service Recovery than their bosses do. Supervisors are often overwhelmed with what's on their plate and often overcompensate because their focus is simply getting something checked off their list so they can attend to other matters. When trained, front line workers provide a more balanced and reasonable service rescue.

Such Service Recovery needs be prefaced with adequate training and coaching. The most powerful example of this comes from the Ritz-Carlton hotel. They are known for empowering employees hundreds of dollars a day per Guest for handling Service Recovery matters. That means that a housekeeper on duty could easily comp a few room nights without ever having to ask their manager. It also means that if they request the assistance of a co-worker to provide that service recovery, they can rely on their co-worker to comply with the request.

This idea isn't exclusive to the pricier hotels. Each year Hampton Inn refunds half of 1 percent of its total room revenue to dissatisfied Guests. In the long run, this pays off for Hampton Inn, because, according to one expert, for every $1 refunded, the hotel gets back an average of $7 in business from a new customer or a dissatisfied one who wouldn't have returned without the refund. Does this happen often? No, not much—their employees are provided tools, such as the ones we've outlined previously, where they are taught when and where to provide appropriate compensation. They also receive coaching as well as daily line-ups where the staff learns from one another. What about customers taking advantage of you or trying to scam you? That happens, but much less than you think. In truth, the industry average is only 1% of any Service Recovery scenario.[7] So don't hesitate to empower the front line. You may see better results than you ever expected. *They* may also help *you* with ideas for Service Recovery. This is highlighted in our next lesson.

LESSON 2: GENERATE LOW/NO-COST SERVICE IDEAS

---

[7] *"Companies give front line employees more power"*, by Gary Stoller, USA Today, 6/26/2005

With so much work on our hands, handling dissatisfied Guests can seem like the last straw on the camel's back. We end up giving away the business, when we really cannot afford to. That's not to say that we shouldn't provide appropriate Service Recovery, even being the "Hero" when an opportunity presents itself. It simply means we should be more creative in terms of identifying what that Service Recovery might look like, rather than dropping back and punting with expensive measures because we haven't got any other solution on hand.

I saw this play out with a particular zoo I worked with. It seemed that they handled Guest concerns by always handing out a free ticket to come back to the zoo. Didn't see the monkeys? Here's a ticket to come back. Didn't like the pizza? Here's a ticket to come back. Looks like it's going to rain? Here's a ticket to come back. The end result was that they nullified the value of attending what was otherwise a terrific zoo. As a team, you should identify ideas for offering low/no-cost Service Recovery to your Guests, whether they are internal or external. One of their solutions when the situation was severe was to provide a 1:1 experience with their dolphins. It was a big wow, and it didn't cost the organization any money.

You may even want to create a contest to reward the individual on your team who comes up with the best idea for Service Recovery. The idea is to provide the best Service Recovery possible at the lowest price. I saw this in action at Disney's first vacation club resort, Disney's Old Key West. They held a contest among their Cast Members: Come up with the best low or no-cost idea for Service Recovery, and win a fantastic grand prize. As I recall, the grand prize was a high-end television or theater system. It was worth a considerable amount of money and the contest was open to all employees with several other prizes involved. The effect was outstanding in that some really creative ideas were brought to the surface—ideas that in turn saved the company tens of thousands of dollars when Service Recovery was needed.

LESSON 3: NET YOUR RECOVERY

Once I hosted a dinner group at a popular Downtown Disney operating partner restaurant followed by the early showing of *La Nouba* at Cirque du Soleil. The decision to have dinner at this location was an easy one. The food tastes great, and its location is ideal—only a few steps to the show. The challenge was that we only had about 90 minutes from arrival to show time. I wasn't told that this would be a particular problem at the time we booked the 20 some participants for dinner. However, as we arrived, the service staff began to show some stress over having to deliver the meal in a timely manner. They offered a three-course meal option to the group, and the end result was that we were running out the door barely having finished the main entrée.

In a display of Service Recovery, management took it upon themselves to make up for the hurried dinner event by hosting us for dessert after the show without cost. That ended up working very nicely as we had a wonderful time chatting about the *La Nouba* show while enjoying dessert on the patio outside the restaurant.

Fast forward to a year later. We took another group of approximately the same size to this same restaurant. It was the first time we'd taken a group there since that previous experience. Only this time we decided to arrive much earlier, giving ourselves over two hours to enjoy the meal and be in our places on time for the show. That being said, nothing had changed. Despite the fact that we did not order from the three-course meal option, the service still took forever. It took well over an hour from the time we ordered the meal to the time it arrived on our plate. In the interim, some received soup or a salad, but many simply sat there the whole time.

Again, I love the food at this restaurant but it took some 40 minutes from being seated to when we ordered, and then over an hour for our entrées to arrive. Our group had to run out at the last minute to catch the show, and many did not have time for dessert or coffee. As before, management came to the rescue: they offered free dessert after the show. Like the zoo example, it seemed as if they had a "one solution fits all" approach to Service Recovery. In this instance, that was not a feasible solution given our schedule. We were unhappy that they had failed to attend to our need of faster service to attend the first *La Nouba* show, although we had made it very clear from the outset. They went back and forth for some time and then they decided on, what I thought was an amazingly poor gesture, to comp the gratuity. I didn't think that our servers were necessarily to blame for the failure to get our food out to us (though one might debate whether they were advocating for us), but for management themselves to offer to give away a portion of their pay seemed incredulous to me.

Finally, they offered the whole meal for free. Comped meals are great, but that was a little over the top as well. We still emphasized the need to pay the gratuity, and did so before we left.

Here's the message: In over a two-year period it became clear that they had dropped back to relying on a "Come back for free dessert" policy rather than fix the problem they had in the first place. Why didn't they simply fix their processes so as to assure a meal in a reasonable time frame? In an earlier chapter, I spoke about Service Netting as opposed to Service Recovery. The emphasis was on the idea that it's better to have a net in place (as in the analogy of a high wire act), than simply to call 911, which is more of a Service Recovery measure. When you offer Service Recovery, and you end up doing it frequently for the same problem, that's a clear indication that you need to create better nets.

In all of this, know that Service Recovery and Service Netting are not easy concepts, but it is where the rubber meets the road. Great organizations succeed when they implement such measures. After all, the magic behind the business isn't some wand or spell, it's the effort you take to create loyal customers day in and day out.

IMPROVING YOUR SERVICE RECOVERY RESPONSE

LOOKING IN YOUR OWN MAGIC MIRROR, ASK YOURSELF:

- AM I EMPOWERING THE FRONT LINE TO MAKE THE RESPONSE?

- IS MY SERVICE RECOVERY RESPONSE IMMEDIATE?

- AM I GENERATING LOW/NO-COST IDEAS FROM MY EMPLOYEES FOR OFFERING SERVICE RECOVERY?

- HAVE I PUT RESPONSES IN PLACE FOR CREATING SERVICE NETS TO AVOID HAVING TO PROVIDE SERVICE RECOVERY IN THE FUTURE?

J. JEFF KOBER

SECTION
III

THE HEART OF SERVICE

Leading the magic requires leading from the heart

"IN ORDER TO MAKE GOOD IN YOUR CHOSEN TASK, IT'S IMPORTANT TO HAVE SOMEONE YOU WANT TO DO IT FOR. THE GREATEST MOMENTS IN LIFE ARE NOT CONCERNED WITH SELFISH ACHIEVEMENTS BUT RATHER WITH THE THINGS WE DO FOR THE PEOPLE WE LOVE AND ESTEEM, AND WHOSE RESPECT WE NEED."

--WALT DISNEY

21

WALKING IN THE SHOES OF GUESTS

LEADERS WALK IN THE SHOES OF OTHERS

No great Guest experience is possible without leaders. When I say leaders, I don't mean managers necessarily. I mean those men and women who step up to the plate to make the magic happen. I've seen leaders in every level of the Disney organization. They inspire all around them, and they make the magic come alive.

There was no better ambassador for the Guest experience than Walt Disney himself. Walt modeled the kind of service brand he wanted from everyone in the organization. He asked that his managers be physically out in the park, not behind a desk. He himself had an apartment built above the firehouse at Disneyland where he would come to visit regularly with his wife and grandchildren when they were not at the Studio. Before the park opened, he would walk the park to make sure everything was in order. During the day he would get out in the park to observe the Guest experience. On some evenings, he would walk up and down the street at midnight pouring coffee for the third shift workers. It was through these efforts he came to know personally what was working, what needed improvement, and how to make it the best experience possible for the Guest.

One day a Jungle Cruise pilot failed to notice that Walt Disney himself had joined the fellow passengers. When Walt stepped off the boat, he walked up to the one of the park's superintendents, Dick Nunis, and asked, "What's the trip time on this ride?" Nunis replied that it was seven minutes. "I just got a four-and-a-half-minute trip," Walt said. "How would you like to go to a movie and have the theater remove a reel in the middle of the picture? Do you realize how much those hippos cost? I want people to see them, not be rushed through a ride by some guy who's bored with his work."

"Could I go on a trip with you?" Nunis asked. He and Walt rode one of the boats through Adventureland and Walt demonstrated how to navigate the experience—"Speed up in the dull stretches, then slow down when you have something to look at." For a full week, the Jungle Boat pilots were timed with stop watches until they perfected the length of the ride. When Walt arrived for his regular visit to Disneyland on a subsequent weekend, he walked through Adventureland without stopping for a ride. He did the same the following weekend. After three weeks, he took a ride on the Jungle Boat. When he returned to the dock, he entered the next boat for another ride. He went around four times, eliminating the possibility that the operators had "stacked the deck" by giving him the best pilots. When he emerged from the fourth trip, he turned to Dick Nunis and gave him a thumbs-up sign.[8]

Since then, that thumbs-up sign has come to represent "great show" in providing quality Guest service in all of the Disney parks.

GET MANAGEMENT OUT IN THE PARK

One of the really great experiences for office management at Disney is the opportunity to work in the parks during the heavy holiday and travel seasons. This tradition, a part of the Disney culture, dates back to early years. It even existed in a similar form during the company holiday party (when the Disney organization was much smaller). At one point this was a single evening after-hours party at the Magic Kingdom at which management served the front line staff. That no longer exists at Walt Disney World, but old-timers discuss it fondly.

Beyond the holiday party, however, management was also expected to be out in the parks, supporting the heavy seasonal crowds. Typically

---

[8] Van Arsdale France, *Windows on Main Street*. 1st ed. Livonia: Stabur Press, Inc.

the scenario during the holidays is for management Cast Members to sign up for a particular responsibility on given dates. Those who had previously worked a given park role could return to that role as long as they had kept their competency current. Such roles might include operating Kilimanjaro Safaris, or driving the Walt Disney World Monorail. The rest of us, especially individuals like me who had never been in a front line position, would be asked to do the simplest of jobs: picking up trash, washing dishes, stocking shelves. Several of my colleagues would do anything to get out of it; personally, I enjoyed it immensely. I loved interacting with the Guests in the park, and would often bring Disney "critters" - those small plastic character figurines - to give away to Guests as the occasion permitted.

The purpose of this activity is four-fold:

First: Bring all hands on deck. With crushing crowds, it is a situation for which everyone is needed to help serve the Guests and assure as much safety as possible for everyone involved.

Second: It's a great way of cutting costs while reducing the need for too many additional seasonal employees.

Third: Managers can learn much about their operation, particularly about how to better engage employees and serve customers.

Fourth: It allows the opportunity for front-line employees to know their job is important enough that salaried managers are willing to cover shifts and help them in the trenches.

HOLDING DOWN THE BRIDGE

I worked many a park shift during my tenure at Disney, but one in particular has always stood out. It was New Year's Eve and I was tasked with helping tidy up at Pinocchio's Village Haus. This consisted largely of cleaning trays and tidying up tables and chairs. I busily carried out this task for several hours until the restaurant started to slow down. Management then asked me to help out along the parade route for a late night run of The Main Street Electrical Parade. I was sent to the bridge at the entrance to Liberty Square. The bridge was designed to be wide enough to handle the influx of Guests coming to and from Liberty Square, but it was not designed to allow parade viewers to line each side of the bridge while the parade passed by. That meant that 30-45 minutes before the parade made its way through, we needed to close off the bridge and tell Guests to travel an alternate route.

Here were the options we would explain to Guests who wanted to cross the bridge:

Option #1: Head back through Liberty Square towards the entrance of Frontierland. Cut through the corridor where the restrooms were, then meander through Adventureland until you came out of that entrance. This option is not a long trek to traverse, but it was difficult to explain to Guests who did not know the park that well and were thus not familiar with those narrow, thematic corridors that linked Frontierland to Adventureland.

Option #2: Turn left, head toward the castle and work your way around. The problem with this is that during the parade there is no real exit back onto Main Street from Cinderella Castle, nor at the Tea Cup corridor straddling Fantasyland and Tomorrowland. Essentially, for this route to be successful, you work your way through Tomorrowland until you can come back through on the opposite side of the hub. This option was particularly grueling for families with small children and strollers.

Did I mention it was New Year's Eve? Holding down the bridge was a challenge. The three of us expended all our efforts explaining to people why they could not come across the bridge as the parade was heading this way. "I just want to exit the park!" was the typical statement, and explaining how to do so was arduous in a mob scene. The two others accompanying me on the bridge had pretty much resorted to pointing towards the path leading to Cinderella Castle. I tried to offer more detailed directions, but it wasn't easy, as many of the Guests spoke no English. Fortunately I am fluent in Spanish and could give explanations to many, but it was still painful. All we could do was to make the best of it.

As this planned chaos swirled around me I kept thinking, "There must be a better way!" The obvious answer was to cut a path or build a bridge directly from that point over to the Adventureland entrance. I made inquiries with parade management as to why we hadn't created a better pathway between the entrance of Liberty Square and the entrance of Adventureland. A small backstage corridor exists for Cast Members, why not Guests? The responses were not satisfying. They ranged anywhere from "that's how it has always been" to "no one upstairs ever listens."

Ugh.

Those responses suggested a culture where employees for that area were not being engaged in resolving customer situations. It suggested an "old school" paradigm of "just do what you're told." I wondered if parade management had ever experienced holding down the bridge? I certainly imagined they had, but how could they have gotten to this point of leaving so many Guests frustrated? I myself had no authority over this area of operation. All I could do as a Cast Member on loan to the Magic Kingdom was to exert my influence and voice my concern to management.

There is a happy ending to this story. It turns out that some 18 months later, a beautiful bridge was constructed between the entrance of Liberty Square and Adventureland. It is a perfect solution for Guests wanting to exit the park from that side of the property without having to go around, or worry about the parade route.

Now I would *like* to say that I had a hand in that bridge being built— but unfortunately, I can take no more credit than I can take credit for the Internet. But I fancy myself as possibly something of a domino in that decision, which was probably supported from annual monies each park is given to improving Guest service. For all my wishes, I would love to see it named after me in the same way other managers get a window on Main Street. We could call it the *Kober Korridor*!

Well...I can dream, can't I?

WALKING IN YOUR CUSTOMER'S SHOES

LOOKING IN YOUR OWN MAGIC MIRROR, ASK YOURSELF:

- AM I, AS A LEADER, WALKING IN THE SHOES OF MY CUSTOMER?

- HOW DO I GET MY MANAGEMENT IN THE TRENCHES WITH MY FRONT-LINE EMPLOYEES?

- DO I HELP SUPPORT CUSTOMER SERVICE AT PEAK TIMES WHEN HELP IS NEEDED?

- AM I ENGAGING EMPLOYEES IN DIALOGUE IN BRINGING OUTSTANDING ISSUES TO THE FOREFRONT AND HELP DEVELOP SOLUTIONS?

- DO EMPLOYEES FEEL THEY CAN TAKE ACTION THEMSELVES, OR IS DECISION MAKING IN THE HANDS OF MANAGEMENT ONLY?

22

LEADING BY EXAMPLE

AT DISNEY, EVERYONE PICKS UP TRASH

"It will never stay clean!" That's what many critics said of Disneyland when it first opened. Even Walt's wife was skeptical that the park would be kept up. "When I started on Disneyland, my wife used to say, 'But why do you want to build an amusement park?'"[9] He wanted to keep the park clean to the point that people would be embarrassed to throw anything on the ground.

Since then, Disneyland has become renowned for being clean, friendly and fun. All Cast Members learn this at Disney Traditions, Disney's infamous employee orientation. The first rule is: "We create happiness." But the second is right behind it: "Everyone picks up trash." Of course, there are wonderful Cast Members assigned to emptying trash receptacles, handling sweeper pans and brooms, and carrying out specific maintenance duties, like changing light bulbs. But no Cast Member, whether a Host for The Great Movie Ride, or an executive vice president, should walk by a leftover napkin, a park map, or an empty water bottle, and not pick it up.

Claudio Diaz, my Disney Traditions trainer, demonstrated modeling this behavior, while we walked the Magic Kingdom that first hot summer day. As we stood in front of Cinderella Castle he modeled this message as he picked up the tiniest pieces of trash out of the planter. The message was clear—*Everyone* picks up trash!

---

[9] *The Quotable Walt Disney,* compiled by Dave Smith. New York: Disney Editions, 2001

CLEANLINESS IS A "KROC"

This way of thinking is not so different from McDonald's.

Over a number of years, McDonald's has been in a marketing partnership with The Walt Disney Company but their relationship goes back much further. Ray Kroc and Walt Disney crossed similar paths as ambulance drivers in World War I. Curiously, both misstated their ages in order to go into the war and serve in the Red Cross. Ultimately, on separate journeys, they both created two of the most recognized companies to ever cater to families the world over.

McDonald's has been known consistently for its logo, look, product, and efficient service. As Kroc tried to create a product that was in tune with the drive-ins of the 1950s, he also focused on maintaining the facilities. Attuned to the quality of the restaurant experience, Ray Kroc was known to tell his employees, "If you've got time to lean, you've got time to clean!"[10]

The emphasis here is not just one of cleanliness. The important message is that, when teams work together to make improvements that positively affect everyone, they become more cohesive. Their pride improves, productivity increases, and quality becomes apparent. Simply said, involvement creates ownership, which leads to employee engagement!

Now I know what you're thinking—we've all been to a McDonald's that's been anything but kept up. Food has been left on the tables, the restrooms are unkempt and the trash receptacles are overflowing.

While this is true of many a McDonald's I've entered, I've also been in several that are fairly outstanding. At the end of the day, it's really about whether leaders take the lead at each location to make their operation the best it can be.

---

[10] Ray Kroc, *McDonald's History* @ McDonalds.com

LEADERS MATTER

Despite the fact that at Disney's annual shareholder's meeting, someone always seems to complain about the bathrooms in the parks --and that consequently the whole organization is going downhill--it is seldom as a whole, that Disney is sliding downhill.

In reality, when it comes to creating priorities, it's about the individual leader. Leaders really do matter. They matter most when they take the reins, when they pick up trash, when they are involved. An operation is no better than its immediate leadership. Leadership for me is many things, but one of the most important is modeling what you want others to do. If you pick up trash, everyone will pick up trash. If you show courtesy to your employees, your employees will be friendlier to your customers. If you take the time to have a little fun, your employees will make it fun for others.

The net effect? It will be cleaner, it will be friendlier, it will be more fun.

Hmm...Clean, friendly, fun. Sounds like something Walt Disney would say.

So wherever you work, make the magic in your business. If you don't know where to start...try picking up the trash!

LEADING BY EXAMPLE

LOOKING IN YOUR OWN MAGIC MIRROR, ASK YOURSELF:

- WHAT DOES "EVERYONE PICKS UP TRASH" LOOK LIKE IN MY ORGANIZATION?

- WHAT IS MY MANTRA FOR EVERYONE BEING ON BOARD?

- WHAT CAN WE BE WORKING ON WHEN WE HAVE "LEANING" TIME?

- DO I MATTER AS A LEADER?

- DO I EXEMPLIFY WHAT I WANT OTHERS TO DO?

- AM I WILLING TO DO EVEN THE TOUGHEST OR MOST MUNDANE JOBS?

23

EVERY EMPLOYEE A GUEST

WHO IS THE MOST IMPORTANT VIP?

There's another twist to the term "Every Guest a VIP"—beside the fact that the *"I"* means Individual as well as Important. Guests are *internal* as well as *external* and must be treated as individuals. Who are internal Guests? Those are the people we serve that are employees of our organization. One Cast Member serving another is as important, if not more important, than serving the external customer, because it all tiers up to the eventual Guest experience. Let's look at an example of this:

Let's suppose I am a Cast Member working the counter of the restaurant at Lottawatta Lodge during lunchtime at Disney's Blizzard Beach. I'm on the front line, responsible for serving a Guest who requests that there be no cheese on her hamburger. So I turn to the cook and request no cheese. Who is the cook serving? Well, ultimately, the cook is serving the Guest wanting no cheese on their burger. But the cook is also serving me as an internal customer: another Cast Member.

The cook is trying to flip that burger, but in goofing around and acting like some "wannabe juggler," the spatula falls on the floor. Usually there would be a clean spatula he could grab quickly, but the dishes are piled up so he heads back to the kitchen sink to clean the spatula he has. In the time that takes, the hamburger is overcooked. But the cook was left with no choice. The staff is short of kitchen help. The manager could come in and help out, but she's on hold on the phone trying to find out from Casting (human resources) why they *still* haven't filled the position for the part-time kitchen person.

Casting is on hold with the manager because their computer system is down. In fact, it's been down several times over the last few weeks, making it increasingly difficult for them to complete the task of hiring a new dishwasher. They've been promised that the hardware glitches would be taken care of, but that requires the support of IT. IT would have had the part available, but in the last calendar year, they purchased so many parts that their budget went over. So in this calendar year there's been a push back in the opposite direction so as not to stock up on those parts. Thus, Casting is waiting until a part comes in.

Why did the budget get cut? That's because a senior head of the organization railed on the IT department for not managing its costs. In part that was justified because IT didn't effectively manage their supply chain. But the senior head went so far as to create an absolute prohibition on obtaining parts until they were needed. And why did the senior executive get on IT's case so badly? There's a promotion he's looking for, and he knows he has to have his ducks in a row in order to lock in on that promotion. The VP he reports to considers having a "perfect budget" as a requirement for promotion—no matter what it takes. Last year's "imperfect" budget was inexcusable and caused the exec to miss promotional opportunities.

And why did the vice president not forgive that senior executive for the budget overrun? In her mind, a perfect Guest experience is ultimately what the Guest wants. And keeping costs low is just one of those ways. Only, you can't create a perfect experience. No one can create a consistently perfect experience. But what you can create is a highly individualized experience.

Well, in this instance what that meant was that the Guest wanted a burger without cheese that wasn't burned. But that's not what happened...the burger was burned. Oh...it wasn't burned that badly. Not so bad that the Guest thought it would be worth bringing the burger back and waiting even longer. Not so bad that she would write some letter to the vice president of Disney. But it was dry. It wasn't very tasty. Was it enough to keep that Guest from *ever* coming back to Walt Disney World? Perhaps not. But the Guest wondered during that time if maybe on their next vacation, they might not spend some of it elsewhere, rather than entirely on Disney property.

LESSONS FROM LOTTAWATTA

Several important messages leap out of this hypothetical, but very plausible, example:

First, consider the Disney expression, *"If you aren't on the front line, then you are the front line to the front line serving the Guest"*. So, in a sense, *every* Cast Member is a front line employee when it comes to serving others.

Second, great organizations succeed when they flip the traditional organizational pyramid upside down and ask themselves, *"What can I do to support those who I work with or who report to me?"* When that occurs, a different experience appears--one that could look like the following:

- The cook focuses on how he can anticipate the needs of the individual on the front line serving the Guest, rather than doing aerial tricks with kitchen utensils.

- The manager is in the kitchen asking how she could support her staff by rolling up her sleeves and going to work in the dish room. She then follows up on the vacant position during an off-hour of the day, rather than during the most important hour when she really needs to be in the trenches.

- Casting proactively leaves the manager a voice or e-mail message explaining they were having difficulties completing the hiring of the Cast Member but that they were working on it rather than the manager having have to go and seek a response.

- IT implements better measures to realistically estimate how many parts are needed in order to best meet the needs of all internal departments they serve, rather than simply over estimating and overstocking.

- The senior executive considers how he can better support IT in estimating its budget rather than submitting a budget based on his own need to get a better position.

- Finally, the VP practices leadership by walking around to determine how she could best support the senior executive in eventually assuming a greater role.

Third and finally, my experience has shown me that the biggest obstacle to greater customer service and loyalty is our inability to take care of and recognize employees within our own organization. For instance, during my business seminars, I ask organizations "What would it be like if, for one week, every person within your organization took the time to pay attention to or recognize someone else in your organization? What would your organizational culture be like?" Answers of "fantastic!" and "phenomenal!" are common, along with "we'd be at the top of our customer service game!" In light of what we've already learned about customer service, these responses reflect the obvious—if you want to take things to another level, you must take the time to understand people and treat each of them as someone special.

And the best way is to treat them like a *VIP*. A Very *Important* Person. A Very *Individual* Person.

DISNEY LEADER BASICS.

In Section II, we spoke about key behaviors expected of every Cast Member. But there are also key behaviors expected of every leader. Again, perhaps leader means manager in some people's mind. But I think that a leader is someone who steps up to the plate in making a great Guest experience.

I lead with a positive attitude and demonstrate commitment to Cast Members.

- Foster a positive and safe work environment.
- Take a sincere interest in Cast Members and make them feel included and valued.
- Treat Cast with the same courtesy we treat our Guests.
- Actively listen to the Cast and quickly follow up on their issues.
- Motivate and engage Cast Members through inspirational

163

leadership and storytelling.

I know and manage my operation and teach it to Cast Members.

- Know when to make decisions and when to empower the Cast.
- Transfer knowledge and skills to Cast Members.
- Monitor, measure and make balanced financial decisions to ensure an efficient operation.
- Be available, visible, and able to assist in the operation as needed.
- Remove barriers and identify improvements in the daily operation.

I recognize and hold Cast Members accountable for delivering the Four Keys Basics.

- Reinforce how Cast Members' actions make a difference for Guests.
- Recognize and appreciate improvement and good performance.
- Consistently and fairly communicate expectations and uphold standards.
- Explain the whys behind decisions.

If you really study this list, there's very little that applies to only managers. This is an opportunity for all to create a great Guest experience. That's why every employee has an opportunity to be a leader. Each individual can actively listen, remove barriers for others, and recognize the good work of others. Not only should every employee be considered a guest. Every employee should be considered a potential leader who influences their team for good.

MAKING YOUR CUSTOMERS VIPS

LOOKING IN YOUR OWN MAGIC MIRROR, ASK YOURSELF:

- WHO ARE MY INTERNAL CUSTOMERS? HOW DO I INDIVIDUALIZE THE SERVICE I PROVIDE TO THEM? DO I UNDERSTAND THEIR BASIC NEEDS?

- HOW DO I TREAT EMPLOYEES LIKE A VERY IMPORTANT PERSON?

- HOW DO I TREAT EMPLOYEES LIKE A VERY INDIVIDUAL PERSON?

- IF I'M NOT ON THE FRONT LINE, WHAT DO I DO TO DIRECTLY SUPPORT THE FRONT LINE?

- HOW CAN I TURN THE ORGANIZATIONAL PYRAMID UPSIDE DOWN TO BETTER SERVE THOSE THAT REPORT TO ME?

- HOW CAN I PLACE GREATER EMPHASIS ON RECOGNIZING THE WORK OF MY EMPLOYEES?

- WHAT BEHAVIORS DO I EXPECT OF OUR LEADERS? OF MYSELF AS A LEADER?

24

THE GIFT OF EMPATHY

GIRAFFES, DINOSAURS & FRIES

Much has been said of customer service. But without that personal care and empathy, nothing comes of it. I define empathy as listening with the heart. It's hard to quantify what creates empathy. I think it comes from the things we spoke of earlier, taking time out individually and giving of one's self. It has much to do with walking in another's shoes.

I have two children who deal with the challenges of autism. One day, I took the youngest, who struggles most, to Disney's Animal Kingdom. He was six at the time with limited language skills. But I knew he wanted to go to the park. And I know that when we go there, we have to do three things: Giraffes, dinosaurs & fries.

As we got out of the car, he grabbed a small toy horse. I directed him to leave it in the car, but he was insistent about bringing it along. I emphasized that he could end up losing it if he brought it. But he insisted in bringing it. We entered the park and headed toward Kilimanjaro Safaris. As we prepared to board the first row of the caravan truck, I took his horse and placed it in my pocket. The last thing we wanted is for a bongo or a zebra to be digesting four-legged plastic.

The truck forged onward with a spirited Cast Member at the helm. Shortly thereafter my son started to whimper.

"Are you okay? What's wrong, son?" I couldn't understand his answer.

We came upon the rhinos and I turned his attention to them: "Look! Rhinos!"

I did the same with the hippos, and then with the crocs. But he was upset and not even wanting to look out. I kept inquiring, "What's wrong?"

We reached the savannah and then he started crying out. I couldn't figure out what was wrong with him. Was he in pain? Was the Cast Member too loud on the speaker? We reached both adult and baby giraffes and I thought, "Surely he'll be excited to see his favorite animal." He didn't pay attention. Mandrills, elephants, and flamingos. I pointed out each and he held no interest like he usually did.

He remained upset and soon started crying. I became frustrated and I kept asking him what's wrong. I couldn't understand him. I felt embarrassed in front of all these Guests with a child that is clearly upset. But I couldn't appease him. He's been on this safari at least three-dozen times in his life, and I had never seen him respond this way.

This continued all the way until we got to Pride Rock setting with the lions, when I suddenly realized—duh—he wanted his horse. I pulled the horse out of my pocket and he was as happy as he could be. Fortunately, we were at the end of the journey, so there was little possibility of it falling out of the safari vehicle. Unfortunately, it kept him from being able to enjoy the many animals we saw.

Thinking through this, I realized I need to do a better job of listening.

We headed toward the other end of the park to DinoLand, U.S.A. Typically, our experience has been to do the TriceraTop Spin as well as The Boneyard playground.

This time, I turned to him and say, "Here we are at DinoLand. Where would you like to go?"

He turned and headed off. He went by The Boneyard. He passed by the TriceraTop Spin. Finally he arrived in front of a fiberglass dinosaur squatting along The Cretaceous Trail. He climbed on top with the other children. I sat on a nearby bench and observed. He spent an easy 20 minutes enjoying climbing all over that dinosaur. Finally I suggested we go find other dinosaurs. We wound our way along The Cretaceous Trail past some other dinosaurs positioned in a way that they cannot be climbed on. We then re-emerged where he took note of the iguanodon positioned in front of DINOSAUR. He made some growling noises. Then he ran as fast as he could. Where to? You guessed it. Back to the original dinosaur he was playing on.

I let him enjoy another 10 minutes playing on this dinosaur contemplating the enjoyment he found from this simple attraction quietly situated in a vast billion-dollar park. I then motioned it was time for us to head out. He had no interest.

I asked, "Would you like some fries?"

"Yes. Fries."

I walked past Restaurantosaurus and PetriFries and headed over to Safari Barbecue. I knew if I got him some fries at the other two locations he would still want to go back to the dinosaurs. I got in the queue at Safari Barbecue. I looked at the children's meal to study the options. They had just recently made an effort to be more nutritious, emphasizing grapes and carrot sticks and apple juice, with a parenthetical statement about cookies, fries and soda being substitutes upon request. I have no problem with this. I think it's a good thing. But I did promise fries, and though they are offered on the menu, fries are not promoted as much as other children's meal options. Over the blare of a nearby percussion band, I asked for fries.

In a thick accent, the international program Cast Member told me it was not an option. I was confused. I asked about the cookie. The Cast Member tells me the cookies are extra. I noted that it's listed on the menu as an option. Against the constant beating of the band, she stated that my choices were grapes, carrots, applesauce and Jell-O.

I asked what "is the cookie and soda a substitution for?"

She didn't understand.

She kept telling me the same thing over: "you may have two choices of the grapes, carrots, Jell-O or apple sauce."

Frustrated, I ordered applesauce and grapes. She rang up the order and I went to the counter. None of the others understood me either. The music was loud and all of them spoke English only as a second language. Against the blare of the band, I tried to explain the confusion to another person at the counter. Seeing my frustration, but not really understanding my actual concern, he gave me a complimentary cookie. I wasn't looking for something free, I was looking to switch. Still no one seemed to have understood.

And of course my son didn't get his fries. Our stay at Disney's Animal Kingdom went downhill at that point.

A LESSON FOR ALL—EVEN CUSTOMERS

Now, what do all three of these experiences suggest? We have to do a better job of listening with empathy, of trying to understand. They say empathy is like an iceberg—it has two parts: The top part above the surface is the skill; the part below the water is our own attitude in understanding others. And that has to be an attitude of the heart.

I'm not blaming the communication skills on someone who speaks English as a second language. I have lived abroad a couple of years struggling to speak Spanish on the streets of Colombia. It's not easy. I empathize. And against the blare of the band, I don't find fault with her any more than I blame my son who is struggling to learn to speak as well. It's simply that most of us—including customers—need to be more patient in understanding and empathizing with others. More than anything, it seems to be about listening more and walking in the shoes of others.

Speaking of shoes, two days later I was getting my son dressed for school. He complained about his shoes being too tight. I loosened the Velcro and repositioned it. He still complained. I adjusted it again and again. He still wined. Frustrated, I yelled out, "then you adjust them!" Upset and bawling, he went looking for mom.

Quickly I defended myself: "I've tried to adjust them. I don't know why he's complaining."

My wife replied, "Well, it would help if you put them on the right feet."

I guess we all have much to learn about listening and empathy.

THE GIFT OF EMPATHY

LOOKING IN YOUR OWN MAGIC MIRROR, ASK YOURSELF:

- WHO ARE THE MOST DIFFICULT CUSTOMERS YOU DEAL WITH?

- WHAT ARE YOU DOING TO BETTER UNDERSTAND AND SERVE THEM?

- AS A CUSTOMER YOURSELF, DO YOU HAVE EMPATHY TOWARDS THOSE WHO SERVE YOU?

- ON A SCALE OF 1-10, WHAT SORT OF EMPATHY DO YOU HAVE TOWARDS THOSE YOU SERVE? WHAT WILL IT TAKE TO MOVE IT UP A NOTCH OR TWO?

25

MAGIC TO THE VERY END

DOUBLE DECKER SERVICE

On our very first trip to Walt Disney World after Thanksgiving of 1988, we spent five days exploring every crook and nanny of what then was only the Magic Kingdom and Epcot. By the last night we were exhausted. We had walked all day. While we budgeted carefully for this trip, we splurged on a formal dinner at L'Originale Alfredo Di Roma in Italy. After a meal and IllumiNations we decided to sit down and enjoy our last moments in the park before the long walk back to the bus section at the front of the park. When it seemed that most everyone had filed out, we began to get up to leave. All of a sudden, out of nowhere came one of the double decker buses that used to circle World Showcase.

"Would you folks love a ride?"

"Would we? Absolutely!" We got on board and soon headed around World Showcase—past Germany, China, Norway and Mexico. We figured he would drop us off at near the Port of Entry stores at entrance to World Showcase. But the jitney took a right turn through Future World and right up to the front of Spaceship Earth. It was a little thing, but how it meant so much to us.

We left our first trip at Walt Disney World on such a positive note. In the years since, we've spent many an evening on a date night at Epcot. We still stand in awe over IllumiNations, and we've enjoyed nearly every restaurant in Epcot. But nothing will compare with that small moment when someone offered us a ride back to the front of the park.

I learned later that those driving the buses were scheduled to close the park, and that they could not go home until the park was cleared of all Guests by security. Since Guests were seated in table service restaurants right up until park closing, Guests were often dining in World Showcase long after IllumiNations, and so the buses would keep running until the restaurants were clear. It didn't help that some Guests were a little inebriated, so getting them back to the front of the park was a chore in and of itself. To support the third shift, which had to wait until security verified the park was clear, the staff of each restaurant kept World Showcase operations informed as to when Guests left each dining location so they could be whisked back to the Epcot exit. Cast Members often enjoyed giving this 1:1 type service, and like us, the Guests were very appreciative of the service.

Certainly it created magic to the very end.

AT THE TIME OF CLOSING

One of the things that Cast Members enjoy most about working at Disney's Animal Kingdom is that the park usually closes sooner than the other three parks at Walt Disney World. Most days, minus summer and special holidays, the park closes at 5:00 pm. That means that many can be home by suppertime. It's a nice perk.

But then comes the long summer when the park closes more around 8:00 pm. Most Cast Members are ready to go home long before that, but many Guests like to come during those last hours of the day since the weather has often cooled off a little from the hotter, stickier moments of the day.

That was my experience with my son when we came around 4:00 pm one day. Now ten years old his itinerary was to see Festival of the Lion King. Mine was to check out the new Wilderness Explorers interactive game. Less technologically based than other interactive activities that had been introduced at Epcot and the Magic Kingdom, I wondered if my autistic child would show interest.

On the bridge leading to Discovery Island, we met up with a very lively Kalah, who handed out books to several children, including mine. She taught all the Caw Caw Roar, handed out the Wilderness Explorer Call Badge sticker and sent all on their way. My son was not the least interested. We tried another stop or so, but his interest was Festival of the Lion King. So we journeyed on to that location.

Afterwards we came to DINOSAUR, his second favorite attraction. Not the ride—just the pre-show. He's yet to do the actual ride. After spending quality time with Phylicia Rashad, he mentioned interest in getting something to eat at Restaurantosaurus. It was about 7:35 pm. I wasn't hungry—I just ordered him a children's meal and waited. And waited.

There were only two or three other people in the restaurant ordering food, but my meal took over ten minutes to come back to us. I watched through the opening in the wall to see what was going on. The Cast Members seemed to be chatting away while waiting for a food product to be readied for another Guest, not thinking about going on to the other orders. When they got around to my order, they pulled out a burger from the steamer, slapped it between two buns and added fries.

I commented on how long I had been waiting to the Cast Member working the counter. She apologized, but offered no explanation.

We sat down and I looked more closely at the meal. Twelve French fries were all that were there at the bottom of the bucket. What was most frustrating was observing the manager on duty, who seemed more concerned about closing up areas of the kitchen and restaurant than making certain that Guests had a great experience.

Given the price, it was disappointing.

My son finished his meal and we left. Heading back to the entrance of Dinoland, U.S.A., we happened to pass by another Wilderness Explorer station where a Cast Member was busy putting things away—after all it was now around 8:00 pm. Suddenly she turned, noticed us, and called out to us. "Hey, I met you earlier today at the bridge when you received your Wilderness Explorers Handbook."

It was Kalah. She gave direct eye contact with my son and invited him again to do the Caw Caw Roar. He wasn't focused on her, and I apologized for his cognitive challenges. But she would not be deterred. She invited him to see the fossils and to name some of the animals displayed there at the Troop Leader Post. Soon he had worked through a very short version of earning the Fossil Badge. I thanked her, and started heading to the exit, when I realized how she was really in no different a position than the cast at Restaurantosaurus. She wanted to get home too. She could have ignored us, or simply waved at us. Instead, she chose to interact.

I found the same thing happening when I reached the bridge at Discovery Island. It was well after closing, but several Wilderness Explorers were helping youth with the final qualifications of their badges.

It's not easy to give your all each and every day when you provide customer service. It's even more difficult when you're exhausted and ready to head home. But sometimes the most important service is offered in the final hours of the day more than any other time of day.

WISHES & TINKER BELL

I also have a daughter who has some challenges with autism. Specifically, when the fireworks go off at the Magic Kingdom, she becomes very frightened. Several years ago when Wishes premiered at the Magic Kingdom, I told the rest of my family that I would take her inside an attraction during that time so they could see it. She was 4 at the time. As the hour came upon us, I moved toward Buzz Lightyear's Space Ranger Spin. She panicked. I didn't realize she was anxious about that attraction as well. Looking hurriedly for somewhere to turn, I ran across the way to The Merchant of Venus. There were several Guests still inside shopping, so I thought I was fine.

That said, within 5 minutes they had all exited, and I knew I still had some 10 minutes to go before the fireworks concluded. The manager on duty at the store informed me that the store was closed. I explained the situation. He and two others on duty, ready to pull their cash till, looked at me like they were going to die if they had to wait another minute to get off duty. But they said nothing. I sort of sunk into a corner with my daughter trying not to cause any difficulty.

The next few minutes were awkward. But finally the fireworks ended and I took her by the hand and headed out the door. I was already moving away from the building when the manager called after me. I turned and looked around. Kneeling in front of my daughter, he said: "Before you leave, we want to give you something. It's a gift from Tinker Bell. She knew you couldn't see her and the fireworks, so she wanted you to have something."

He handed her a Tinker Bell wand, which lit up in the night. Fascinated, she clutched on to it watching it change many colors. Thanking him profusely, I thought to myself: "Yes! He did the right thing! He created a Take 5 moment for my child out of what was an awkward situation!"

On my way out of the park, I had to tell someone, so I stopped at City Hall. Keep in mind, I stood before a Hostess who looked exhausted from the day's whining. You could see she was just going through the motions of hearing another complaint. When I got to the part where the young manager gave the Tinker Bell wand, you could see her do a double take. "He did what? That's wonderful! What's his name? We'll have to thank him!" I acknowledged him and continued on my journey. Sharing my experience with another brought perhaps more joy to her than it did to my daughter.

The power of service is a funny thing. It's very magical. In truth there was no requirement, no protocol, no expectation or service recovery. It wasn't Disney's fault that my daughter was afraid of the sound of fireworks. Yet that young man became the hero that evening. A hero. That's the power of service.

And more often then not, it comes at the very end of your shift.

CREATING MAGIC TO THE VERY END

LOOKING IN YOUR OWN MAGIC MIRROR, ASK YOURSELF:

- WHAT IS THE FINALE OF YOUR GUEST EXPERIENCE?

- HOW DO YOU SUSTAIN THE GUEST EXPERIENCE THROUGHOUT?

- HOW DO YOU SUPPORT YOUR EMPLOYEES IN SUSTAINING THE GUEST EXPERIENCE?

- WHERE ARE YOU AT CLOSING? HOW DO YOU KEEP THE MAGIC GOING?

26

SERVICE VS. "SERVE US"

CREATING YOUR OWN WONDERFUL WORLD OF SERVICE

Perhaps you read this book hoping you could make your organization as customer friendly as Disney's. Perhaps you just want to take the organization to the next level, and you want some fresh ideas. To this end this book is dedicated.

Having taken this journey, here are the lessons I believe that are at the heart of creating a great Guest experience:

- "Bump the Lamp" in your own business
- Understand others
- Walk in the shoes of others
- Get everyone on board with your vision
- Build on values and standards
- Align your behaviors to your values
- Greet everyone you meet
- Smile
- Help people find their way
- Model what you ask others to do
- Put your best face on when in front of others
- Catch others before they make an error
- Give customers the power to make choices
- Give the gift of time
- Make the wait worthwhile—or don't let them wait at all
- Be a hero

- Listen and apologize
- Make others feel special
- Treat others like Very Important and Very Individual People
- Look for high tech/high experiences
- Show empathy

It's been my good fortune to see individuals and organizations take these ideas and bring them into their own corporate culture. For the most part, the experience is really quite magical. Not because there was some dose of pixie dust, but rather because people's hearts were changed.

But these philosophies are not only good business sense, they're good rules to live by in life. Because at the core of all of this is not "serve us" but rather "service." Any time we take on the act of serving others, magical things really begin to happen.

There's a quote that has been at the heart of my own personal philosophy for many years. It came written on a bookmark, a small gift given me when I was a young man laboring to help others on the streets of Colombia. In English, it reads:

> *I slept and dreamt that life was joy*
> *I awoke and found that life was service.*
> *I acted, and behold, service was joy.*

> --Rabindranath Tagore

So here's to the magic of serving others—whatever that may look like in your organization, in your life. Here's to creating your own wonderful world of customer service!

See you at the parks!

Jeff

Index

THE WONDERFUL WORLD OF
CUSTOMER SERVICE AT DISNEY

WHAT'S YOUR NEXT STEP?

ORGANIZATIONS JUST LIKE YOURS ARE TRYING TO FIGURE OUT HOW TO CREATE SERVICE MAGIC IN THEIR OWN ORGANIZATIONS. JEFF HAS WORKED WITH A WIDE VARIETY OF ORGANIZATIONS IN THE PRIVATE, PUBLIC AND NON-PROFIT SECTORS TO HELP THEM ACHIEVE EXCELLENCE IN CUSTOMER SERVICE, LEADERSHIP, EMPLOYEE ENGAGEMENT AND TEAMWORK.

NEED A KEYNOTE SPEAKER? INTERESTED IN A WORKSHOP OR SEMINAR? HOW ABOUT A UNIQUE PROGRAM THAT VISITS BEST-IN-BUSINESS ORGANIZATIONS TO LEARN THEIR SECRETS FOR CREATING WORLD-CLASS EXCELLENCE? BEYOND PROGRAMS, JEFF PROVIDES CONSULTING, ORGANIZATIONAL DEVELOPMENT, INSTRUCTIONAL DESIGN, AND SO MUCH MORE.

FROM HOSPITALS TO GOVERNMENT AGENCIES; FROM BANKS TO ZOOS; FROM ASSOCIATIONS TO UNIVERSITIES, JEFF HAS LABORED FOR SOME THIRTY YEARS TO HELP ORGANIZATIONS TAKE THEIR WORK TO THE NEXT LEVEL. AND HE CAN HELP YOU DO THE SAME.

YOU'LL ALSO WANT TO CHECK OUT OTHER BOOKS, WRITINGS AND APPS AVAILABLE FROM PERFORMANCE JOURNEYS. TO FIND OUT MORE, VISIT:

PERFORMANCEJOURNEYS.COM

YOU CAN ALSO CONTACT JEFF AT 407-973-3219, OR AT JKOBER@PERFORMANCEJOURNEYS.COM

CALL TODAY! LET US KNOW HOW WE CAN SUPPORT YOUR ORGANIZATION MOVING FORWARD.

Made in the USA
Coppell, TX
27 September 2022

83700687R00108